The Innkeeper's Diary

By Pamela Collins

© 2014 by Pamela Collins

THE INNKEEPER'S DIARY

Dedication

I want to say sincerely how much I appreciate my editor Suzanne Doukas for her patience and help with writing this book; To my stepdaughter Kelly, thank you for following your intuition and saving Christopher's and my life; To Russell for showing me hell so I could recognize heaven; For my guardian angels who intervened a time or two; For the people who read my very rough drafts and they know who they are; For my wonderful little nuns and monks at the Holy Nativity Convent and the Holy Transfiguration Monastery for lighting candles unceasingly when I got into trouble and started to lose faith; To my little angel girls, Jaeda and Cambria, whose lives are just starting, but I am sure they too, will become lights to others as they grow; To Rod who let me babysit Cayden for a week with nothing to do, so that I could begin writing this biography; To my family who gave me such great characters to write about; And a huge 'thank you' to my dear friend Dianne who talked me into writing a book even if it wasn't the comedy she had in mind.

I am dedicating this book to the men in my life; Father Isaac, Christopher, Jonathan, and Marcus who are truly the valves that lead directly to my heart and keep it beating.

And finally, I dedicate this to my patron saint, the Theotokos, the Virgin Mary, and mother of the Lord, whose hand has clearly been on my shoulder throughout my life.

Table of Contents

Introduction — 2

Prologue: Russell — 3

Chapter 1: The Bag Lady — 17

Chapter 2: Genesis — 23

    Pappou and Yiayia 23

    Dad's Family 25

    Mom's Family 26
        Aunt Aggie 26
        Aunt Betty 30
        Gust 31
        Aunt Clee 32
        Aunt Clee's Death 35
        Aunt Chris 36
        Uncle Tony and Uncle Ernie 36

    Mom and Dad 38

Chapter 3: Growing Up in Utah — 43

    Early Days 43

    School 44

    Sweet Sixteen and More Than Kissed 46

    Rome Adventure Starring Jacqueline Bisset 50

Chapter 4: Angels on My Shoulder — 58

Chapter 5: Life as a Single Mother — 63

    The Wish List – Education and Edification 63

    The Farmhouse 65

    The Monk and the Miraculous 67

Chapter 6: A New Life in Boston — 75

    The Original Boston Rascal 75

A Friend and a Father 77

If Only 80

Congressman Kennedy 89

"Hello. I'm Joe" 91

Chapter 7: The Mask of Death   98

My Father's Conversion 98

The Miracle Christmas 101

Dad's Premonition 107

Chapter 8: Heaven, Hell and Hollywood   110

My Happy Place 110

Blair and the Red Flags 113

Kindred Spirits 122

Loss of Another Kind 128

Chapter 9: Birth of a Notion   135

Kicking the Habit 135

Finally Home 137

History and Mystery 139

Tools of my Trade 141

Sally, Oh Sally 143

The Doc 147

An Inn is Born 149

Be My Guest 152

If There's a Will, There's a Way 161

Chapter 10: Kismet   167

Two Strangers at an Airport 167

The Virtual Date 170

Chapter 11: The Moneychangers   **175**

    Heavenward 175

    Bank Lending 178

Chapter 12: Living History   **186**

    Captain's Row 186

    Doc was Right 189

    God Provides – Does He Ever! 193

Chapter 13: On the Waves of Change   **198**

    More Answered Prayers 198

    Sea Story 204

Chapter 14: Revelations   **208**

Epilogue   **210**

Endnotes   **213**

Introduction

Dear Reader,

We are, all, the creators of our stories and our lives - up to a point! Our free will is limited by events that are not always in our control. I have been exploring why things happen and what control I have over them for the past 45 years, only to conclude that there is a truly mysterious, wonderful and unseen world out there, and we should not be so ready to discount it.

I wanted to capture some of the strange, beautiful, ugly, and miraculous events that I have experienced in my life and how, at times, I have left this world we call *normal* and experienced things that came from somewhere else, somewhere other, somewhere unseen. If it were not for my husband, my editor, and reviewers, this compilation and collaboration of my life's journals and notes would still be stashed in a box in the basement.

As you read I hope you keep an open mind and consider all the possibilities of existence, because, what is real to one person may indeed seem unreal to another.

I know this to be true.

Pamela Collins
June 2015

Prologue: Russell

The year before I started my first college course, I lost my husband to a self-inflicted gunshot wound. He was handsome, creative, and charming. He was also angry, abusive, and controlling.

Russell and I met in 1978 in Utah when I was twenty-one years old. I had gone with a group of girlfriends to ladies' night at a local discotheque in Salt Lake City; not to drink but to dance. Russell stood at the bar with a beer in his hand, checking out the women as they passed by. He was the best-looking guy in the place, maybe even the whole city! He was stunningly attractive in the very classic tall, dark, and handsome sort of way. As the night went on, he spotted me across the room, laughing and talking with my friends. He eventually made his way over to our table and we began to talk.

While we were talking, I was overcome by a strange premonition. I intuited, which is the only way to describe it, that we would be together, but for only a brief time, that our relationship would end tragically and, of all things, it would happen for my own good.

It wasn't as though premonitions were new to me. It wasn't the first I'd ever had and wouldn't be the last – as I found later. Throughout my life I had extraordinary experiences, but never understood why. I once asked a priest about the feelings, thoughts, and visions I had and was quite surprised when he said it was just psychological -- basically, all in my head. He said only saints and the great ascetics were given those powers. The answer just did not feel right. I knew I was no saint - not by a long shot - but I felt connected to something more profound, more mystical, and more loving than life itself.

There had to be another explanation as to why I had a vision years ago of how my first teenage love would die. I remember the scene in my mind's eye; him lying unconscious on a bed in our friend's apartment. At the time, an incredible sadness overcame me. I didn't understand what it was, and never entertained the idea that it wasn't just my imagination. Then, two years later, he was found dead from a heroin overdose, on the bed in the apartment of our friend. My heart sank and my stomach turned to ice when I found out.

So, I wasn't too surprised when I had the premonition about the man I had just met in the disco, but was surprised by what it told me. We talked and flirted for the rest of the night. Before we parted ways, he asked me to go out with him the next night. I said, "Yes." Are you kidding? He was so handsome!

I was ready by seven o'clock and waiting for him to show for our date. I waited and waited and waited. After a while, I realized that I had been stood-up. I had known women who hung around at home waiting for their never-show-boyfriends to come by and I always thought they were rather crazy to do it. But I had never been stood-up before! And I had a big enough ego to think, *who does he think he is to do that to me?!* That thought and my bruised ego are the only reasons I can offer as to why I agreed to give him a second chance.

On our first date (the one he showed up for) he took me to one of the ski resorts in the area for dinner. We ordered our meals, had a few drinks and talked about ourselves to each other as people are want to do on their first date. Soon after we finished eating, he excused himself and went to the men's room. I patiently waited, holding on to the next thought I wanted to share with him when he returned. Several minutes went by and I began to look around the room trying to spot him. Several more minutes went by, but he still didn't come back. I sat and waited several minutes more. This had never happened to me before so I was unsure what it meant or what to do next. Then, as I was about to pay the bill and leave, he returned to the table.

He confided that he used to take beautiful women to restaurants and leave them there without so much as a "so long." He said he decided not to do that to me because I wasn't stuck up like the others. I guess I was supposed to be flattered. I now realize that that was my first - well, maybe my second - sign he was a creep. But I was young and inexperienced with men like Russell. He was attractive, funny, and very romantic. I fell in love with him so fast I barely remembered what life was like before him. It was only after I married him that I learned he had beaten his first wife.

After we married, he was a thoughtful, caring sort of friend and lover. He always helped people with their construction projects; homes, sheds, decks. He even helped strangers on the side of the road if they were stuck in snow. He had a charisma that seemed to emanate from him. Everyone loved being around him. He was a proud, doting father to his daughter from his first marriage. I would watch him as his face would brighten, become more handsome, if possible, whenever she walked into the room. It was an amazing display of pure, uncomplicated love. But it was not long after that the full realization of who my husband was and what he was capable of became painfully, dangerously evident.

We settled down in Salt Lake City, Utah, in a farmhouse my parents owned. Soon after we moved in, my cousin gave me a beautiful white Labrador puppy - just a month old. His name was Sam. He was undoubtedly my favorite wedding present - soft, playful, and loving. Everywhere I went he went, dancing around my feet waiting for my attention. Sam kept me company and helped with chores on the farm while Russell worked on the Union Pacific railroad as an engineer, leaving me alone three or four days a week at a time.

Sam and I would get up early in the morning and make our way to the barn to feed and water the horses. And though he was small and hardly worth noticing, he would scamper around, jump wildly and bark at the legs of the horses, which always made me laugh. It reminded me of the mouse that roared. The horses of course could not have cared less about his shenanigans. They would merely nudge him with their noses and give him a gentle push here and there – just so he knew who was really in charge. I sensed we all knew it was all in good fun. The truth is, Sam and the horses developed a nice little friendship.

I had Sam for only a few short weeks before he began to throw-up and walk a little odd. I assumed he ate something rancid in the barn, such as a dead mouse or bird. After a couple days, when he did not get any better, I took him to the veterinary hospital. The doctor examined him and told me that Sam had contracted canine Parvovirus; a highly contagious, potentially fatal virus. The recommended treatment was very expensive and I had no idea how we would pay for it. I told the vet I could not make a decision just then and would need to discuss it with my husband. So, feeling heartbroken, I gathered up the puppy, and left.

When I got home, I sat at the kitchen table with Sam in my lap as I told Russell about the virus, the prognosis, and the cost. I explained that it would cost a thousand dollars to save the puppy or, alternatively, it would cost two hundred dollars to have him "put to sleep" (a conscience-sparing euphemism for death). Russell did not react and I could not read his face; it was expressionless. He just sat there. He didn't say, "Yes" and he didn't say, "No." Eventually, got up from the table and left the room. The decision about my puppy seemed to have been put on hold for the time being.

Later that night, while I was cleaning the kitchen after dinner, Sam at my feet, Russell came in the room, grabbed the puppy, and put him in a brown grocery bag. Confused, I asked what he was doing. He didn't answer. He calmly carried the bag out to the patio. The bag bulged and crinkled as the puppy squirmed to escape. Then, the man I married, the man I shared my bed and my dreams with raised his arm high over his head and with hammer in hand, brought it down on the bag. Horrified, I screamed for him to stop! Over and over and over again I screamed. The whole scene took on such a surreal quality I found it difficult to believe I was actually there, that it was real. The dog was screaming and I was screaming. In my mind's eye, I had horrible visions of what the poor thing was going through trapped in that bag. From somewhere far away, I found myself in motion. I grabbed Russell's arm and tried to pull him away. After a several moments of struggle, I finally succeeded, but, to my horror, I was too late - or too soon. Sam, inside the bloodied bag, was barely moving but still alive. Nauseous and in shock, I retreated to the house. He then pounded the bag over and over until it became obvious that the puppy was dead. Afterward, he buried the remains in the backyard. We never spoke of Sam again.

As our life together continued, the only time I really saw Russell happy anymore was when he was with his daughter. He was a different man; cheerier, kinder, and devoted. I thought perhaps if we had a child of our own, his demons would go away and he'd be more contented. We could be the happy, loving family we both said we wanted to be. And so, two years after we were married, Christopher was born and I found I was very much mistaken.

I don't know when or how it happened, but I saw less and less of the man I loved and more and more of the thing he had become. Time and time again I found myself the focus of his frustration and anger, which was a very scary and intimidating place to be. At times, he would make me sit at the kitchen table with him, night after night, hour upon hour, while he smoked his Marlboros and drank coffee –

cup after cup after cup. All the while he'd be telling me how worthless I was, a terrible mother, a bad cook, and a selfish woman. He said I was a horrible human being and a bad lover, that no other man would ever want me so I'd better not plan on leaving him—*ever!*

Another time he found me in the bathroom getting ready for work. I had begun modeling for extra money and was dressing for a fashion show. Without a word or forewarning he pushed me up against the cinderblock wall and slammed my head against it again and again. Why? I don't know. One of the most unnerving aspects of his abuse was that he did not need provocation or a reason - not one that I could ever ascertain or avoid, in any case. I didn't make it to the show that night. And how I ever got through that abusive evening, I'll never know. Why I didn't pack up and leave was an even bigger mystery still.

When Russell's violent episodes went into remission, as they sometimes would, we continued to build a life together. It was during one of these lulls that we purchased a house in Sandy, Utah in a suburban cul-de-sac. We were so excited to be new homeowners. And I suppose to our new neighbors our little family seemed happy, healthy, and, -dare I say it - normal. I was, however, growing less and less able to keep up the facade. It made me sick to make love to my husband. I felt it was my obligation as his wife so I never said, no. Instead I would just lie there waiting, hoping for it to be over sooner than later. I had given up even trying to make him think I enjoyed it. The pretense had become emotionally draining and caused me to despise myself more than I despised him. I was raised to believe that my vows were a commitment to God as well as to Russell, so I tried to be the dutiful wife - for better or for worse and all that. I kept praying and waiting, thinking that since I was married in the church and lived according to their rules, God would make things better. Though, I must confess, I'd often think He was taking His own sweet time doing it!

Once we settled into our new home and lives, it didn't take long for us to notice that the neighborhood was crawling with cats. It seemed as though everyone on the block had at least one. Cats of all shapes, sizes, and colors would hang around the yard - prowling, peeing, and pooping. But of all the annoying behaviors they had, the one thing that really set Russell off was when the cats would climb up onto his Porsche at night and sleep on the hood. He would come in the house after catching a cat sunning itself on his car and scream and yell obscenities – at the cat, the neighbors, and me. It bothered him so much he devised a way to trap them in the garage and then get "rid of them."

His M.O. would be to open the garage door, place some fish at the back and sit for hours, waiting for a cat - attracted by the smell - to come in. Once inside, he would pull the door closed behind it. As they scurried about trying to escape, he would shoot at them with his bow and arrow, using them for target practice. The trapped felines became a sort of sadistic sport for him.

Other times, after trapping a cat in the garage, he would skip the play and just drown them in a barrel of motor oil and once they were dead, he would bury them in the backyard. After a while, and to my horror, our yard had become a preternatural pet cemetery.

The neighbors I'm sure, had no idea where their pets were or what had become of them. Every once in a while, though, a "Have you seen my cat?" flier would be posted on a telephone pole. I was so terrified of my husband I could not bring myself to tell anyone what was happening. But, at the same time, I could not let things continue as they had been. So, I called the police anonymously and told them that there was a crazy man in our neighborhood hurting animals. I asked that they put out a bulletin to alert people so they could take precautions and protect their pets. I'm not sure my efforts saved anyone's cat but it brought the reality of my dysfunctional marriage and husband into keen focus. My son would not grow up witnessing such horrors. I made up my mind to *get out!*

The end of my discontented life arrived shortly afterward. We, as a family, had gone grocery shopping together. When we arrived home, we busily unpacked the car and brought the bags into the house. Everything appeared to be well. It was just a pleasant family day. My son Christopher, who was eighteen months old by then, played in the living room as I went upstairs to our second-floor kitchen to put the groceries away. As I unpacked the bags, putting the items in the cupboards, I turned to see my husband standing behind me, pointing at a ring of chocolate milk on the counter.

"Why is this not wiped up?!" he screamed. His face was distorted with a grotesque rage that did not fit the apparent crime.

Before I had time to react or even understand what was coming next, Russell grabbed me by the hair with one hand and by the throat with the other. I struggled against his grip. It made him squeeze harder. I was sure I was about to die -- over spilt milk, no less. While I struggled to breathe and maintain consciousness, from far off I could hear Christopher crying. My last thought before I passed out was, *'Oh my God, what is he going to do to the baby?'* When I came to, I was lying at the bottom of the stairs that lead to the kitchen. It took me several seconds to realize that I had fallen over the upstairs balcony and landed on the floor below. Looking up, I saw my baby boy sitting at the top of the stairs crying uncontrollably. He evidently had climbed up to the kitchen to see what all the commotion was about. The idea of my son witnessing such violence against his mother was somehow worse than the abuse I endured. Without a second thought, I calmly got up, climbed the stairs, picked up my baby, called my mother and left.

I spent several years in therapy, afterward, trying to understand what was wrong with *me*. Why would I choose to marry such a beast? What made me stay after witnessing and experiencing his cruelty? The questions kept coming, and they were painful. It took a long time to identify the cause of my low self-esteem, and even longer to correct it. I couldn't understand what made people act the way Russ did. But I knew I had been living with evil. Was it pure evil from hell itself or was it a man choosing to act evil? This was the singular point where my future was to be decided. I desperately needed angels now to defeat the demons.

Shortly after our separation, I received a phone call from the Emergency Room at Alta View Hospital. They told me they were admitting Russell for attempted suicide. Someone driving up Little Cottonwood Canyon Road in Wasatch-Cache National Forest found him crawling in the middle of street, presumably, hoping to be run over by an unsuspecting motorist. After some convincing, they were able to get him in the car and took him to the hospital. The nurse on the other end of the phone said Russell was asking for me and wanted to know if I would come. I told her I wanted nothing to do with him and to call his brothers.

A few hours later his brother called and begged me to come to the hospital. I told him, "No. I am free of Russell and his insanity!"

A short while later, I received more calls from the hospital and from his brother. It seems Russell was pulling the needles and tubes from his body and attempting to walk out of the hospital because I wouldn't come to see him. Eventually, and against my better judgment, I agreed to go.

As I arrived at the hospital, I saw police cars with lights flashing, an ambulance, and a struggle in the parking lot. I soon recognized Russell's brother and I stopped the car and hopped out. There were four emergency medical technicians and a policeman struggling against Russell's, seemingly, superhuman strength. They were all trying get him secured on a gurney. A nurse circled the chaotic scene of moving arms, legs, and bodies in order to find an opportunity to inject him with a tranquilizer. After they finally got him calmed down and strapped in, I saw, what I can only describe as a mad man. He was unshaven and sweating profusely, his hair was wet, slick and matted to his head. I had never seen anyone look so pitiful. And though you would think he deserved no pity for the awful things he had done, it hurt me to watch it.

Russell lay on the gurney looking up at me and crying pathetically. In that moment he had the deepest, saddest eyes I had ever seen. At that moment, I felt nothing but pity for him. I saw him struggling to free himself, just as I imagined my little dog struggled to free itself from the punishing brown paper bag. He pleaded, "Please, Pam, please don't let them do this to me." For someone who needed to control others, this, I believe, was the worse fate of all.

I walked up to his room with his brother and I explained that I was never going back to Russell, the divorce would soon be final and he was theirs, meaning his family's, problem now, not mine. As I drove away from the hospital, I was unexpectedly filled with tears and compassion remembering the sight of such a wretched human being. I prayed to God to forgive him and bring him peace.

The last time I saw Russell alive, he called and asked me to give him a ride to his antique store - a business he started after going to a few auctions in England. Always a sucker for someone in need I reluctantly agreed.

As we rode along, we started to argue. I really don't remember what it was about. The sad fact about our relationship is it never really needed to be about anything, just a situation he wanted to control. Maybe it was the sight of me sitting in the driver's seat that agitated him. I was no longer intimidated by his aggressiveness. He could no longer control me. This was my car and he was a guest in it. I refused to kowtow to him or shrink from his ranting. He suddenly grew very angry and threw his hot cup of coffee in my face, pulled my hair, and slapped me again and again. I struggled with the steering wheel to keep from driving off the road. The car behind us honked furiously. They could see what was happening and felt it was all they could do to help me. Russell yelled for me to pull down the next street (it was a very secluded area). I refused and kept driving. I was determined that he was not going to be my captor anymore.

A little further down the road I saw a police car with a policeman standing next to a car and talking to the driver. I pulled up alongside them and with coffee dripping from my hair, I told the cop that my passenger was abusing me. By this point, Russ was so out of control, he just continued yelling and screaming at me. The officer told Russell to get out of the car and put his hands behind his back. Utterly surprising to me, he did as he was told, was handcuffed, arrested, and put in the back of the police cruiser. The officer advised me to go straight to the courthouse and file a restraining order, which made me anxious. It seemed to me that so many of the women who took that advice were found dead afterward. Though I suppose it isn't the restraining order but the reason you need one in the first place that is the common denominator.

The next day, I took Christopher to my parents' house. I told them I was going out of town for a few days and asked them to watch over my son. I never discussed my ordeal with Russ with them so they were unaware of the fear I lived with. Then, with my son safe and sound at my parent's, I went to stay at a women's shelter in Salt Lake for a week, just until I was sure Russell had cooled down and would not come to my house to finish what he started.

The nights I spent in the shelter were enlightening. The women who shared the bond of abuse also shared their stories. I was surprised to find that for many women, this was not their first stay. They were stuck in a cycle of loving and leaving their abusers. There were even accounts of women who had been killed by their violent partners after leaving the shelter. I did not feel safe during this period but I eventually returned to my child, my home, and my life. So, with restraining order in hand and Mom and Dad two doors down, I knew the hold Russell had over my life had come to an end.

Several months later, I was working as a waitress at La Caille in Salt Lake City, a beautiful 5-star restaurant in a French Chateau' nestled at the foot of the canyon. One evening I got called away from my table to answer the phone at the Hostess' stand. It was Russell's brother. He told me that they had found Russell's body in Death Valley with a gunshot wound between his eyes. He told me the coroner's office would like me to call in the morning to describe any scars, birthmarks, or other unusual markings for identification. My knees buckled and I dropped to the floor. The hostess supported me from behind and helped me up. I leaned against the Hostess' podium and began to cry. The middle of a room, full of hungry diners was not the best place to have a meltdown, so she walked me to the lounge where I phoned my sister. My brother-in-law answered the phone and told me her wasn't home. I asked him to have her come and drive me home. I was in no shape to drive. I waited and waited for her until the restaurant closed. Another waitress was leaving and she offered to take me home. The next day I found out that my sister never received my message.

It was a strange brew of emotions that surfaced after Russell's death. His family didn't know where to have a funeral so I said I would make arrangements with my church. I felt as though it was the least I could do for him now.

During the funeral, I sat in the church feeling shock and guilt, two emotions I struggled with to understand. He was a cruel and violent man, so why was it such a shock that his violence had turned on him? And why my guilt? He was my nemesis when he should have been my partner. He was my tormentor when he should have been my comforter. Did I not have the right, the responsibility to save myself and my son?

I went deep inside myself in search of answers. Then, something unexpected and profound happened. I can only explain it as one of those rare moments of clarity when you feel your guardian angel standing right beside you. It was an unshakeable, overpowering sense of conviction that I was at a fork in the road. I knew absolutely that I had two choices; I could accept the blame and believe I was good for nothing and for no one and choose to be devastated and go downhill from there. Or, I could choose to be strong, have faith, and know with all the certainty of my being that things were going to get better. It was *my choice*!

I chose faith and vowed to live a better life. I could feel my inner strength shoring up my resolve. The soul I had pushed down into the darkness for so long suddenly emerged like the uncaged bird. I had been given freedom. Unbelievably, I was overcome by an incredible calmness I never thought possible. I then did something I had not been able to do in the seven years of my marriage. I forgave Russell.

The pain of those seven years had now turned to complete peace, even ecstasy. From that moment on, my senses were heightened; raw with the experience of color, taste, and sound. I was in awe of my new existence in the world. I slept better. I laughed easier. I loved more. I was at total peace within my being. Just as for every action there is an equal and opposite reaction, for all the suffering we endure in this world, one day, one moment, it all disappears and there is a beautiful embracing love and light that words cannot describe.

It was finally over.

Life to me, after that, made complete sense. I was no longer living in a world of torment. I no longer judged. My consciousness seemed to move to another, higher level. I could almost hear the thoughts of other people. I could see pain in a stranger's eyes. I felt who was connecting with the divine and who was not. It was a visceral kind of knowing that amazed and humbled me.

Khalil Gibran wrote that pain is the breaking of the shell to understanding. My shell had been broken and I saw things in a clearer light. I started moving closer and closer to my Creator. It was as though I had given painful birth to a beautiful new life.

I continued to wear my wedding ring after Russell's death. It gave me some comfort and reminded me to never marry again. Besides, I hadn't decided what to do with it yet and was afraid I would lose it. And I did.

It happened when I was in a bathroom in Park City one warm, sunny weekend. I had taken it off and set it on the sink to wash my hands. It wasn't until I got home that I realized I had left it in the public bathroom sitting on the sink. I figured there was no sense in going back. It was gold and probably worth something at a pawn shop. Chalking up the loss to the best laid plans of mice and men, I resigned myself to the fact that sometimes in life, decisions are taken out of your hands, or in this instance, off your hands.

Months later, as I was backing out of the driveway on my way to work, I was overwhelmed by a feeling. I recognized it immediately. It was an intense feeling of loss. At that moment I missed my ring, in a very heartbroken sort of way, and keenly wished I had gone back for it. I stopped the car and sat stewing in my emotions when I abruptly remembered that I left the water running in the backyard. Putting the car in park, I hopped out and walked to the side of the house. As I reached down to turn the spigot off, a glimmer of light twinkling in the dirt caught my eye. Curious, I bent down and brushed at the earth to see what it was. Then, I saw it. It was my wedding ring. I didn't understand how that could even be possible. But I had learned, time and time again, not to question the gifts we are given, just accept them for what they are and say, thank you.

I have told this story to many people over the years, and they always try to logically explain how a ring I had left sitting on a sink in a public bathroom in Park City could end up in my possession once again. And though I listen politely, they will never change what I already know; it was given back to me by the man who gave it to me.

Later that same year, Christopher and I returned home after celebrating his birthday at my parent's house. He had fun and received plenty of presents and lots of balloons. But getting all his loot into the house in one trip was a challenge. So, while I took the presents, he took the balloons. He held them tightly by the strings and guided them from the car to the house. But, before he could get them to the door, his grip on the stings came loose and they escaped. Bobbing and dancing on the wind, they floated out of reach. He wailed and cried as we watched them drift away into the blue sky. I tried to console him by telling him they were going up to see God but he didn't care. He wanted *his* balloons.

A few hours later, the balloons long forgotten, we headed out to the car to go to the store. I held Christopher's hand as he descended the stairs from the house. I looked down to watch each of his steps lest he trip and fall. When he got outside, he looked up and pointed. I followed the trajectory of his little finger, my eyes traveling to the ceiling of the carport, where, to my amazement and Christopher's delight, the birthday balloons bounced and weaved. He was so happy he didn't even ask for an explanation but I let him know that it was his daddy who brought them back from heaven just for him, which I wholeheartedly believe.

I believe the events of my life have provided me with a unique view of this world and the hereafter that not everyone has the opportunity to experience. And it was at this point in my life, after Russell, that I began my search to understand what it was that made people good or evil, or both. I questioned; are we born one way or the other, or do we choose? I wanted to know more than ever what was happening in the unseen world - the spiritual world.

Russell and me shortly after we were married

My favorite picture of my son Christopher and me

Chapter 1: The Bag Lady

As the years passed, the Holy Spirit filled Xenia with greater riches, and she became increasingly blessed. After a while, some people started to notice that "crazy Xenia" wasn't so crazy after all, but was an instrument of divine grace, to whom had been given deep spiritual powers: she could see into people's hearts and into the past and future, and appeared to people in visions. Anyone whom she touched was blessed. Because she gave up living for herself, she was able to live for others, helping those in need. - <u>Life of St. Xenia of Petersburg</u> by Jane M. deVyver

It was a hot, August afternoon; I didn't have any Bed and Breakfast guests for the next few days so I boarded the ferry from Hull, Massachusetts[i], and went into Boston. It was hot and humid; a perfect day to be on the Common. By the time I got there, it was crowded with a variety of people. The disparity between Boston and Utah, where I grew up, with the Mormon Ward houses – all identical - on every block, amazed me. In Utah you would never find the different variety of churches such as Catholic, Methodist, Congregationalist, Synagogues, and Universalists - which you find in Boston. In Utah, even the people looked cloned—all blonde and beautiful. Here in Boston it was totally different. The sights, sounds, energy, history, and culture surrounded me with a strange sort of hum of happiness.

I loved the charm of New England, with all the big beautiful trees, the old-world architecture of the buildings, even the smell of diesel oil and noise of squeaking trains of the Massachusetts Transit Authority - the MTA or the 'T' as the Bostonians call it. When I was in the city, I loved to ride the T. Sometimes, if I were lucky, I would get to hear great musicians in the underground stations. One time, I saw an attractive black man playing an electric violin for tips. His music was ethereal. As I listened, I thought he must be a graduate student or a professor of music. I walked over and glanced at some of his pre-recorded tapes and tossed a few dollars into the opened old violin case sitting at his feet. I may have been underground but the beautiful music sounded as it if were descending from heaven.

I ascended the stairs to the park, and after browsing through the stores in the area, I found a park bench near a large statue facing Tremont Street. I breathed in the heat of the day and the rich smell of roasted nuts from the cart vendor, a mixture of cashews and almonds. It wasn't long before the aroma worked its way into my thoughts and I decided I had to have some. I left my spot on the bench to buy a bag. They were warm, salty, and sweet and tasted wonderful.

I returned to my perch and watched as people went on about their day. I admired the men, how great they looked in their beautifully tailored suits and their air of confidence. It must be nice, I thought, to feel you have the world at your feet. Out west, I grew up amongst cowboys and farmers. The only time I saw a man in a suit was at a funeral or a wedding. I was not making judgments, mind you, it was just different.

The women, to me, seemed odd. I got the sense that they were all trying to be men. They dressed in business suits as well, but wore sneakers instead of stilettos or dress shoes. I didn't understand that at all. That is, until I had started working in Boston in an office and attempted to dress like a 'lady.' I learned quickly and painfully that the cobblestone sidewalks and brick roads were not conducive to wearing pointed heels. Once, I even walked right out of my shoe; the heel lodging itself between two cobblestones. Though I tried to be graceful about losing my footwear in public, a handsomely dressed man, who had been walking behind me, bent down, pulled it out, and handed it to me. Embarrassed, but recognizing the humor in the situation, I smiled and said, "Just call me Cinderella!"

We both laughed and went our separate ways. I don't recall wearing heels again after that. Instead, I opted for a nice pair of flats. I still would not be caught dead in sneakers and a dress.

Sitting in the sun, eating my warm almonds and watching the locals and the tourists pass by was as good as it gets for entertainment. Off in the distance, a stage was being set up for an outdoor concert. The afternoon air was intensely humid and hot but, surprisingly, I was not uncomfortable. I loved studying the people and absorbing all the sights and sounds of such a historic place.

After a few minutes the oddest of female human creatures approached a garbage bin just across from where I sat. She leaned over into the bin and retrieved the remains of a half-eaten chicken sandwich. Her head was covered in an old, ratty, monastic-like black habit. I knew it was a Christian habit because of the red, faded, embroidered cross on the forehead of the veil. She wore layers of old black cloaks. Insane, I thought, in this extreme heat.

After rummaging a bit more in the dumpster, she sat at the end of my bench without appearing to know that I was there. It made me feel a bit uneasy. She then slowly, carefully, and methodically unwrapped the chicken sandwich, looked towards the sky, and then proceeded to rub the chicken skin on her arms and face. After she anointed herself, she took very small pieces of bread and started to feed the birds.

They came from everywhere. Tiny sparrows landed on her as a small child would climb onto a mother's lap. There they waited patiently for their share of bread. To me, it was reminiscent of the scene in Mary Poppins, where the old bag lady sits on the steps of St. Paul's Cathedral feeding the birds. I was still trying to adjust to the fact that she had smeared chicken grease on her skin when she caught my questioning look. I saw in her, the most incredible, peaceful ocean-green eyes. There was more peace, content, and sweetness in those eyes than I had ever seen in human form before. I guessed her to be in her seventies, but she had the eyes of a young woman, which belied her true age. She smiled warmly at me and I felt an incredible lightness of heart.

Then, out of nowhere, a large seagull swooped down from behind her and tried to take food from one of the little sparrows. She shooed the gull away. I heard her tell the little bird, as she stroked the frail birds' neck, "You see, little one, there is always something lurking behind you, waiting to take away your treasure. But there is also a great protection!"

Soon, young dancers appeared on a stage that had been set up in the park. The musicians tuning their instruments played various unmelodic notes as they warmed up for the performance. The old woman and I separately watched the activity on the stage for a moment.

As if reading my mind, she spoke, "They're with the Boston Ballet and Boston Symphony. There is a free concert here tonight. Isn't it all so beautiful?"

I just looked at her wondering if it were wise to respond to such an obvious nut! Should I be polite and start a conversation with someone who wears layers of clothing and a black head covering in the oppressive heat; who probably lives on the streets, and uses chicken grease as body lotion? (I seriously doubted that that was the secret ingredient in perfumed lotions!)

Then the musicians started playing a beautiful melody. "I love this piece," she said "It's Rachmaninoff's Third Concerto. It was featured in Somewhere in Time. That was one of my favorite movies."

She paused. I was still wondering how to respond.

"That happens, you know," she continued, "being able to see through time, and into different dimensional planes. People live here on earth, on different planes. Sometimes you see them—sometimes you don't. It all depends on whether you're on the same frequency!"

That's it, I thought, she just confirmed to me that she is quite utterly nuts. And, yet, I was completely captivated. She continued speaking. I found her voice so sweet, so calming, so pure.

She talked about how much she loved this concerto; how music brings both life and emotion to the soul, and that it is good and bad. "Music carries its own vibrational fields, which can create peace in the brain or agitation on the synapses," she said. "The music we listen to affects our health and serves as a buffer or catalyst to the dream world. The Vegas nerve sends sensory information to the brain, our heart rate tracks the mood of the music, thus affecting our behavior."

"Did you know that the Egyptians used sound frequencies to heal while the Navy uses it to kill?" She asked.

I still did not answer.

The dancers on the stage had fallen into a beautiful harmony of movement when two attractive men in a deep discussion walked in front of us. It seemed as though they were in a political or legal conversation of great importance. Suddenly, one of the men tripped and fell, striking his head on the park fountain, rendering him unconscious. And though unconscious, his eyes remained wide open and, oddly, full of panic. Passersby just stared, not offering assistance. The other mam he had been walking with just moments before, pulled his phone from his pocket and called for help.

The old woman released the tiny bird she had been stroking and got up from her seat. She walked slowly over to the injured man - who now had blood streaming from below his ear - knelt down beside him and lifted his head gently into her lap, as to give him a pillow from the hard ground.

Some people winced as they watched; here was a handsome, well-dressed man in the arms of a smelly, wretched old woman. She held him tenderly. And while she held him, her breathing changed, her demeanor changed, and I heard faint whispers coming from her. I couldn't quite make it out. It sounded like some sort of chant or prayer. She spoke with her head turned towards heaven and talked as though there was someone there with her.

The man's friend finished his call and turned to attend to the injured man. He saw the old woman holding his friend's head in her lapped and gasped, seemingly in fear, as though she were some vulture about to eat a carcass. He abruptly pulled the woman away and kicked her in the side, as if she were a dog, and shouted for her to get away from him.

I instantly and intensely felt the shallow vanity that surrounded the world. I realized how ugly the ego was at any given moment, under any circumstance - the ego so wicked – and yet the heart, so simple.

As the old woman pulled herself up from the ground, she looked into the eyes of her attacker, then returned to her place on the bench. She continued to break crumbs from the sandwich and hold them for the gathering sparrows. She smiled as she watched the EMTs load the injured man into the ambulance. His friend turned and looked at the woman once again before he left. You could see malice in his eyes. She returned his glance with one of the most loving smiles I'd ever seen.

This woman aroused my curiosity. Who the hell was she? How brave of her to care for and comfort a stranger and the boldness of her in the face of the cruel man. All this character from a bag lady! She now made me feel comfortable, so I didn't stop myself from asking, "Are you okay?"

She stared into the distance. While holding her wounded side she answered with a sweet reflective voice, "It doesn't do any good to get angry. A man feels no better for it. Anger is, really, a tormented soul. When the storm of passion has cleared, it leaves him to see that he's been a fool, and has made himself a fool in the eyes of others. The ancient people called anger short madness, because it is such a headstrong and impetuous passion, that there is no difference between an angry man and a madman while in a fit; both are void of reason and blind, at the time."

She folded her hands in her lap, smiled again, and became quiet. I had to know what brought the sweet bag lady here, to the state of being a homeless drifter; although a lovely one.

"It's all about choices," she said, though, I never even posed the question.

"The first choice we make is, what we choose to think about. Then, if we think often about the same things, they eventually become our actions. Our actions form our character, and then our destiny. My thoughts brought me here just as your thoughts have led you here. Even the great saints and monks know this. That is why they follow a strict rule: 'Guard your thoughts.' I suppose your mother had thoughts about getting out of the world she grew up in, so she could create her own destiny in the world of finance and be able to care for her siblings. We can never overestimate the power of purpose and will. The indomitable will, the inflexible purpose looking for the future good through the present evil, have always produced confidence and commanded success, while the opposite leads to depression, disappointment and disaster. When a child is learning to walk, if you can induce the little one to keep its eyes fixed on any point in advance, it will usually navigate to that point without falling: but distract its attention by word or act and down goes the baby. Your aunts' and your uncles' thoughts and their choices led them to their destinies as well, just as those around you, are the result of your thoughts and your choices."

Okay, great, but what did she know about my family? I didn't know this woman from Adam.

Or did I mean -- Eve?

Chapter 2: Genesis

There is neither Jew nor Greek, there is neither slave nor free, there is no male and female, for you are all one in Christ Jesus. - Galatians 3:28

Pappou and Yiayia

My grandfather, James or Pappou (Greek for grandfather), came to America from the isle of Crete with his brother George in 1909. He was 38 years old. They were not exactly young men but it was their only hope to escape poverty after the great current crop failure of 1907[ii]. They left behind their mother, father, sister, aunts and uncles. They were separated from all the family they had known and loved.

Once in America, Pappou and George settled down in Carbon County, Utah where the coal and copper companies were bustling. There was plenty of work in the mines and the company hired many immigrants new to the Country, including my grandfather and his brother. They worked in the Castle Gate coal mines, close to where they lived.

Working in the coal mines was, and still is, a dangerous occupation. One of my family's favorite stories is of the day Pappou and George decided to play hooky from work. Instead of going into the dark hole in the ground for the day, they went fishing in the warm sunshine. It turned out to be an auspicious decision. That very same day, while they were casting their poles in hopes of catching some trout, there was a series of explosions in the mine – three to be exact. Sadly, all 171 men and boys working in the mine that day were killed. It took nine days to recover the bodies. Identification, in some cases, was only possible by recognizing familiar articles of clothing. It is strange and gives me a sense of fate to think that if Pappou and his brother had not ditched work to go fishing, they would have died and I would never have been born.

After the mine collapse, Pappou took whatever money he had saved, and bought several acres of land and a few sheep to herd. He knew about raising goats and sheep from the mountainsides of Crete and, I imagine, the mountainous region of Carbon County felt like home to him. His herd eventually grew to 793 head.

In America as it was in Greece, the coffee house was where all the Greek men congregated. It was, for them, a man's true home to be among other men. The Mormons, however, found the Greeks and their customs to be strange. And the Greeks, in turn, thought the Mormons' practice of polygamy to be sinful and just another version of the Turkish harems. So, in order to keep their customs (and their opinions) to themselves, the Greek's opened their own coffee shops and restaurants.

There were not, however, a lot of Greek women in the small mining towns in Utah. A lot of the Greek men began to marry "picture brides," which were women who were selected to for marriage based solely on a photograph from their families in the homeland. My grandmother, Yiayia, was one of them. What Yiayia thought of this arrangement can only be speculated. I suppose, however that she went along with the custom and viewed it as her obligation and duty, as many women of her generation did.

My grandparents had a small adobe house up in the mountains with one bedroom for ten people -- eight children and two adults -- and a tiny kitchen with a wood burning stove, open cupboards, and a cast-iron sink. They were very poor and heated the house with log fires. Bathing was accomplished in the middle of the kitchen in an oversized tin tub, with water heated from the stove. There was no money and there was no privacy.

For young Greek mothers, life was a continual cycle of childbearing and unending work and my Yiayia was no exception. My mother, the last in the line, had once told me that she would often hear her mother crying and begging for my grandfather to leave her alone, not to have sex with her. They could not afford any more children and she did not want them. In order to provide for the home and children, Yiayia washed other people's clothes by hand and sold vegetables from her garden. Life was so hard on the family that of all the children, only my mother finished high school and graduated with a diploma.

Dad's Family

My father's family on his mother's side was my favorite side of the family. They were farmers, mostly, and Mormons.

The Hansens came over from Denmark and joined the Mormon Church. But, not long after they arrived in Utah, polygamy became a common practice in the Mormon faith - much to the dismay of my great-grandmother. Mads Hansen, my great-grandfather, told her it was part of their new faith and, in order to be a good Mormon, they had to practice what they preached. Well, Great-grandma Hansen wanted no part of it. She would eventually pack up her children and go back to Denmark. Mads, wanting to be a good Mormon, went on to marry a few other women.

One of his wives gave birth to my grandmother, Carrie, who died of breast cancer before I was born. Her sister, Aunt Ollie Mae, became my much loved, de facto grandmother. My parents would take us to her house on Thanksgiving. She always made everyone feel welcome and loved. After a tasty turkey dinner, the children were responsible for clearing the table and washing the dishes. And if we did a splendid job, we would get 'clean plate prize' - her homemade chocolate cake! It was worth every last dirty dish.

My Grandpa was an Irish immigrant who came from County Cavan Ireland to work on the Union Pacific Railroad with the Chinese. He was a Catholic but, according to the family tale, when he arrived in Utah he had to join the Mormon Church in order to get water while he labored. One of his relatives was James Farley, the 53rd Postmaster General of the U.S. under President Roosevelt.

When we went to visit Uncle Junior (my father's brother) on his farm, my siblings and I would hang out on the tractor in the field. We'd sit in the driver's seat and pretend we were the farmers, cutting the hay and getting it ready for market. When I remember these times, I can still feel the sunshine on my face, the smell of the earth and freshly cut summer grass. To this day, if I am driving down the road and my neighbor is mowing his lawn, I am transported back to my uncle's farm, and it always makes me smile.

In the winter, we'd ride sleds after the snow fell on the hills. In the spring we'd go horseback riding in the budding fields. In the summer we'd go waterskiing or swimming in the nearby lake. There was always fun to be had when we visited Uncle Junior's farm, no matter the time of year.

One of my first experiences with cooking was watching my Aunt Hanna, Uncle Junior's wife, bake goods with fresh-milk from the cows. Her cakes and chocolate candies made from cream were the stuff of children's dreams.

The highlight of the year in the Hansen family was the family reunion. We all played yard games, ran races and made up contests. The amazing thing was that everyone got involved, not just the children. Life with them was so much simpler and fun.

It is with everlasting gratitude that I was given the opportunity to get to know and love nature and life in this manner. And I will always love my father for giving it to me.

Mom's Family

While my mother was working hard and earning acclaim in the business world, most of her brothers and sisters were living in poverty. They had never moved far from the little two room adobe house in the mountains of Utah and a few had health issues that prevented them from working. Mom would often dip into her own savings to help them pay their bills, or she'd take time out of her work schedule to guide them through the bureaucratic process of applying for government assistance. Sometimes, she'd even let them, with their children, come and live with us for a while - just until they could get back on their feet, as they would often say.

Aunt Aggie

I considered my mother's sister 'Aggie' the epitome of a strong woman. She weathered heartbreak upon heartache but never let it change her spirit. She was undoubtedly my favorite aunt from my mom's side of the family. It is only now, from the perspective of an adult that I can understand and appreciate all she went through, which makes me admire her all the more.

Aunt Aggie had Tony and Connie from her first marriage when she was just seventeen, and at the age of nineteen, she met and had an affair with a young man named Dick. His claim to fame was being one of the grandsons of the McCoy's - of the famous Hatfield and McCoy clan from Kentucky. They married and had two children, Mike and Wayne. After four children and years of acrimony, they divorced. He, as it turned out, was an abusive alcoholic, and a pedophile.

Dick had visitation rights for his two boys, Mike and Wayne, who were two and four years old at the time of the divorce. Every other Friday, Dick was allowed to come pick up the boys and take them to his apartment for the weekend. And every Sunday night, he'd bring them home. Then, one Sunday night, he didn't. My aunt waited all night until it became apparent that they weren't coming home, then she called the police.

Time ticked by slowly. Days became weeks, weeks became months, and months became years. The FBI took over the case from the local police but they weren't able to locate Dick or the boys, either. It seemed a foregone conclusion that he had taken them out of state. And with 49 to choose from, that was a lot of ground to cover. After years of anguish and no leads, she decided to take matters into her own hands. Borrowing money from my mother, she hired a private detective. It was an expense and a gamble she couldn't really afford but then, as a mother, she couldn't afford not to, either. Thankfully, the gamble paid off. The private detective eventually tracked them to New Mexico where they lived with Dick's brother Morris.

Aggie made arrangements for someone to watch Connie and Tony while she went to New Mexico with the detective. Once there, they called the local police and let them know that they had two kidnapped boys in their town. When they, Aunt Aggie, the detective, and the police, got to the home where the boys had been living, they knocked on the door and waited. The unsuspecting woman who answered was taken by surprise when, out of sheer anger and years of frustration, my Aunt Aggie lunged for her and began tearing at her hair.

Wayne, now four years old, was found inside the house, was put in the car, and taken to the police station. Aunt Aggie remained with Wayne while the detective and the police drove to the local elementary school to retrieve Mike, who was, by then, six years old and in first grade. As fate would have it at the same time Mike was being reunited with his brother and mother at the police station, their father was being hauled in wearing handcuffs. The boys were young adults by the time Dick got out of jail for kidnapping them.

When the boys finally resurfaced they were rather traumatized and had a hard time adjusting. They did poorly in school and got into trouble with the police. They seemed to be struggling with their place in the world and there wasn't much my aunt could do about it, except watch.

Years later, Wayne, the youngest, like his mother, went to work in the mines. Aunt Aggie was proud that her son had followed in her footsteps (and not his father's) and seemed to be making a life for himself when the mine he was working in collapsed. He was 20 only years old when he died.

Tragedy struck again several years later when my cousin Tony, Aunt Aggie's other son, was diagnosed with melanoma. Through multiple surgeries and chemo therapy, Aunt Aggie maintained her faith and would tell everyone who asked that he was fine, and would be fine. Though, this was not true in the end. Tony died of cancer when he was in his early 30s.

Mike, Wayne's older brother, took on odd jobs here and there but never seemed able to stabilize his life. He had two sons by two failed relationships, began using drugs, and became addicted to Methamphetamines. So, while men his age were building careers, getting married, and having children, he was living with my aunt and stealing from friends, family, and strangers just to buy his next fix. He died from hypothermia while wandering in the Rocky Mountains in the dead of winter. He was found completely naked in the snow. He was 45 years old.

When Aunt Aggie met and married my Uncle Ted, she and the family could not have been happier. I thought he was the only man, other than my father, who looked more like John Wayne than John Wayne. I wouldn't be too surprised if John Wayne's cowboy character was developed after a chance meeting of the two of them - cowboy hat, swagger, stance-- and all! He was so kind and sweet that I thought of him as a marshmallow.

Uncle Ted didn't work but owned thousands of acres of land in the Rocky Mountains, which he leased to sheep and cattle ranchers. The money Uncle Ted collected was put aside for his and Aunt Aggie's retirement. She had certainly earned that promise of relief after a life of struggle.

For her part, she continued to work in the coal mines and that provided the couple with an extra income and health insurance. They had a written agreement that she would hand over her paycheck each week, minus a stipend for personal expenses, to my uncle who would use the money to pay the mortgage and other bills. In return, she would inherit his estate – land, stock investments, and all. Uncle Ted had no children so it was not as if there would be anyone to complain about the arrangement.

Then came the bad news. Uncle Ted had cancer. It was an aggressive cancer and he would never see retirement. It was very difficult for Aunt Aggie to relive the surgeries and the chemo treatments that she had once endured with her son. They were both under a lot of stress and it erupted into huge fight - and it was a doozy. It caused such a riff in their marriage that Uncle Ted moved out of my aunt's house and in with his nephew and his wife. Things went on like that for a while until, just two short months later, he was dead.

It wasn't until after he died and the will was read that my aunt learned he had signed over his land and most everything he owned to his nephew. Aunt Aggie was inconsolable and heartsick. The only thing she had left to show for their life together and their plans for the future was a box full of ashes.

One night, after a good, long cry, she took his ashes, given to her in a plain cardboard funeral carton, walked into the bathroom, opened the lid to the toilet, upended the box, pulled the lever and sent Uncle Ted down the tank!

Despite all those years of trauma, she still maintained her love for life and her sense of humor, telling jokes, and giving me a welcoming smile whenever I walked in the door. And, if I ever dared to complain about the traumatic things in my life, she would say to me, "Oh, get over it! It's happened and there isn't a damn thing you can do to change it, except GET OVER IT!"

It wasn't what I wanted to hear at the time but I now know she was right. You can choose to whine and moan about life and the bad things that happen or you can accept that it is all part of God's plan, accept it, get over it and move on.

Not long after losing her husband and her inheritance, my aunt had a stroke. She went to live with her only surviving child, my cousin Connie. Like my aunt, she weathered the tragedies that beset her family with heart and gumption. With good sense and grace from God, she never left the small town of Price, Utah. She raised her beautiful daughter Tracy, who won the title of Miss Teen Utah and was first runner-up for Miss U.S.A. in 1996. Tracy is now happily married and living in Texas. She is a news anchor on her area's local network. Her son Billy became an executive with Utah Power and Light.

Aunt Betty

My Aunt Betty was my mother's oldest sibling. She married my Uncle Marion and had two boys with him. My only memory of my uncle, though, is going to the prison to visit him with my Mom and Aunt Betty. I was very young so I did not understand the situation.

The adults in the family never talked about Uncle Marion in front of us kids so we never knew why he was there. His crime did get him some coverage in the Salt Lake Tribune but we were too young to read it. Now, from an adult perspective, I can only surmise that it must have been a pretty serious crime to land him in the slammer for all those years.

As for Aunt Betty, I never felt comfortable around her. She was the oldest child in the Karterkis family and she smelled funny; not that one thing had anything to do with the other, it was just an unpleasant coincidence. When my mother would take us kids along to visit, Aunt Betty would serve us Greek food, like dolmades (stuffed grape leaves) and spanakopita (spinach pie), which I found dreadful. To make matters worse, her kitchen was filthy, grease, grime, and dirty dishes were everywhere. To this day. I dislike Greek food. And I'm Greek!

Today, Aunt Betty would be called a hoarder. Her house was crammed full of television sets, recording devices, cassette tapes, stacks of old newspapers, bric-a-brac, books, clothes, boxes, and who knows what else. Any flat surface was a good place for something. The bathroom was small and dirty like the rest of the house. On the floor by the toilet were stacks of my cousin Georgie's pornographic magazines and books. Whenever my aunt was asked about the risqué reading material, she would nonchalantly say, "Oh, those are just his books...like Time magazines and such." I'm sure he told her that he "read them for the articles."

As I got older, I would not go with my mother to visit my aunt. But I did hear that their pile of stuff had grown so much that it was escaping the bounds of the house and spilling out onto the lawn and into the yard. Eventually, the neighbors had enough, and called the city to complain. The public works department sent a few men in a large truck to remove all the debris on the lawn, but, to the best of my knowledge, they never did anything about the inside. I suppose it was like that until the day she died. Whatever possessed, or obsessed her to keep all that stuff, to have an uncontrollable attachment to things is a mystery to me. But one thing I know for sure, when Death comes a knockin', he sure as hell isn't going to let you take it with you.

Gust

Aunt Betty's older son, Gust, followed in his father's footsteps - all the way to prison. Long before identity theft was an everyday occurrence, as it is today, my cousin Gust recognized the value of personal data (birth records, social security numbers, etc.) and how to steal it from unsuspecting victims.

For whatever reason, people trusted him, which is a requirement for being a con man I suppose. I mean, you never hear people say, "I never trusted that guy!" after being cheated out of their life's savings, do you? The thing about people like Gust, they really don't have any qualms about who they steal from. They will take from friend, family, and foe alike. It is all about the scam, the 'gotcha.'

One time, early in his 'career,' Gust stole a stack of checks from a girl he had been dating (sounds like my luck) and went to a local used car dealership and bought a Cadillac. With keys in hand and a dealer plate on back, he headed to Oregon. Once there, he gave one of our cousins' a call, someone he hadn't seen in years, to let him know he was in town. Graciously and trustingly, he was invited to stay for a few nights with him and his family. Then, while they were away at work, leaving Gust to help himself to their hospitality, he helped himself to their personal papers. Ruffling through their belongings, he snagged social security numbers, birth records, bank accounts, and handwritten signatures, and started his very own crime wave. It was months before my cousin and his banks found out what Gust had done. To the best of my knowledge, he was never arrested for what he had done to my cousin and his family.

Even my parents, who were very savvy in business and finance, were taken in by him. One time, before anyone knew about the episode with my cousin in Oregon, Gust came to visit Mom and Dad. Like most people, they loved to see family and were happy to see him show up on at their door. With him was a briefcase full of gem stones and jewelry, he told them that they were worth tens of thousands of dollars, but he'd bought them at a fraction of their true value; and what's more, there would be more coming in the mail. Unfortunately, however, he needed to pay for them now and he was a little short of funds. What to do? What to do? It seemed to hang in the air until he asked my parents if they would be willing to wire the funds to the man with the goods, to an address in California. If they could see their way clear to do this for him, they could pick up the box from the post office and keep the valuables until he paid them back. And, if he didn't come up with the money, well then, they had just made themselves a handsome little profit. My parents agreed and went to the post office the next day to pay cash-on-delivery (COD) for the package. When they got it home, they were beyond furious to find that they had paid $10,000 for an empty box. To this day, I can't believe my father didn't take the shotgun to him.

Gust is currently serving a life sentence in California for identity theft and other crimes involving fraud. He is said to be one of the first criminals to get in on the ground floor of identity theft that has caused so much pain and grief for millions of people.

Aunt Clee

Mom's sister Clee was a psychic, and a pretty good one. Aunt Clee's abilities seem to have started when she was a child, after having a vision in the mountains of Utah.

She was a card reader. Not tarot cards, mind you -- regular playing cards! Whenever we went to visit Aunt Clee, she would 'read' cards for my Mom. I remember them both sitting across from each other at the table, the cards laid out between them. I could see from watching them that what the cards told my aunt, and what she told my mother, was serious stuff, though I never really heard the details.

Aunt Clee also read cards for friends and strangers. All types of people came to her house to have their futures divined. There was usually a line and a wait to get in to see her.

One of her clients was one of the primary doctors working on the artificial heart program at the University of Utah. Why he came to my aunt and what she told him was never discussed. My aunt did not divulge other people's lives or what she learned from their reading - almost like a HIPPA law for psychics. In that way, I guess, the doctor and she shared the same professional ethic.

The unexplained and the unknown was always part of my family's heritage. My grandfather Pappou "read bones" for the miners working in the mountains of Utah. Reading bones is a form of divination, as is card reading. It consists of shaking chicken bones in a bag and tossing them into a circle. I don't know who my grandfather learned to read bones from or whether it was a practice he brought with him from the old world, but I do know, somewhere in the Utah coal miner's history archives is a story about 'Crazy Jim" the sheepherder who read bones. That sheepherding bone-reader was my grandfather.

Aunt Clee was always dressed to the nines, as the saying goes. She had jet black hair and looked like Elizabeth Taylor. Like her sisters, she had a few husbands. Her first one, Paul, was a fighter pilot who left her when the children were still small. Her son, Paul Jr., was drafted and sent to Viet Nam when he was 18 years old and did not come back quite right. Before he was drafted, he was funny and loved to play cards and poker. After he got out of the Army, he never adjusted to his post-war life and ended up on drugs. And, in a twisted turn of fate, as if he had not endured enough, Paul lost both his sons to tragic deaths. Anthony, a quiet and gentle soul took off with his teenage friends one night, stole a car, and was driving over 100 mph towards Las Vegas when they hit a semi-trailer head-on. The accident was so bad that the newspapers reported it as the worst in the history of Nevada. His other son was involved in a horrible motorcycle accident and while he was on life support, both his parents were in jail, trying to get out of jail so they could sign papers taking him off life support to send him back to the Lord. My boys

Christopher and Jonathan sat with him in the hospital and wouldn't leave his side.

Aunt Clee's older daughter, Georgia, my cousin, was a Go-Go dancer. If you aren't old enough to know what that is, it is a dancer in a bar who wears tassels over her nipples so you aren't totally nude. Georgia was very pretty and kind but had a hard life growing up, and like other women in the family, married a man who beat her...severely.

I was about seven years old the night my mother got a call from Aunt Clee. She asked my mother to meet her at Georgia's house, immediately. Something had awful had happened. When we arrived at Georgia's house, there were police everywhere – inside the house and out. My mother told them who we were and they allowed us in. Once inside, we followed the commotion to the back bedroom. When we entered the room, I saw blood all over the bed and splattered on the headboard and walls. Her husband, Sam, had been shot in the head as he slept! The smell of it – the blood, and what I now believe was death - made me so sick, I ran into the bathroom, and threw up in the toilet. When I think back on it, I can't believe the police actually let my mother and me - a little kid – into the house or see such a gruesome crime scene. Sometimes, when I'm watching TV, the graphic images shown on crime shows today remind me of the scene in Georgia's bedroom. And I am struck with how horrible it was to witness such a thing, and with how awful it is that such things have become *entertainment* for the general public.

After the police did their investigation, my cousin Georgia was arrested for murder. According to them, she was their prime suspect. (I suppose the spouse always is.) But, to everyone's relief, Georgia was ultimately released and all charges were dropped. As it turned out, Sam had been having an affair with the neighbor's wife. So, when the neighbor's husband found out, he took a gun, a silencer, and the law into his own hands. He snuck into the house and into the bedroom where Sam slept and shot him.

I don't think poor Georgia ever fully recovered from the events of that night. Apparently, she had been lying in bed next to him the night he was murdered. It was probably his penchant for beating his wife, and his blood all over her that caused the police to suspect her in the first place.

Aunt Clee's Death

Opening a door from our world to the next can have real-life, unexpected, and horrifying consequences. I believe my Aunt Clee ultimately found that out.

When my Aunt Clee died, my cousin Paul, her son, was with me. He had come over to my little farm to help with the yard work. We were digging a hole for a pond when he got a call from Georgia. She told Paul that their mother had just died and he should come home. It was not unexpected; she had Alzheimer's and her body was beginning to shut down. In fact, Hospice had been visiting her for weeks and was there when she passed.

When we arrived at Georgia's house, we let ourselves in. As we came around the corner to the living room, we saw Georgia sitting on the couch next to her deceased mother. A large industrial size box of kitty litter was at her feet. The oddity of the kitty litter in the living room, within kicking distance of Aunt Clee's foot, had barely registered once we shifted our gaze from the litter box to Aunt Clee.

There my aunt sat - bolt upright on the couch. Her eyes were wide open, and her mouth was agape and twisted, her face was frozen in terror and in death. I was shocked at the sight of her, but I didn't say anything because I didn't want to bring attention to it - just in case they hadn't noticed. Though how could they not? Still, no one mentioned it, so neither did I.

After I recovered from the shock of Aunt Clee's appearance, Georgia, who seemed amazingly calm considering the horrifying way her mother passed, told us that there was an unbearably ghastly odor coming from Aunt Clee when she died. She described the odor as putrefying. It was the Hospice nurse who told Georgia to buffer the smell with kitty litter until the mortuary arrived. She said the nurse had told her that the physiological systems can create an odor at the time of death, and though it is rare, it is possible. I thought she was just being kind and it was all bullshit.

For me, the events of Aunt Clee's demise reaffirmed what I have learned and believe; that there are malevolent spirits and evil entities trying to enter our world and our lives. I believe that Aunt Clee, a practicing psychic all her life, had been visited by evil before she passed and that that was her last psychic event. Since that day, I have never sought the counsel of psychics and have committed to staying as far away from psychics as humanly possible. Some things you should not go looking for, lest they find you.

Aunt Chris

My Aunt Chris was very sweet and also read cards. Until the day she was reading a fortune and a blackbird flew head-on into her storm door window, breaking its neck and dying instantly. She took that as an omen and never read cards again.   As children we would visit her with our mother. I remember that she would makes us kids butter and sugar sandwiches. I always thought that they were so delicious because she had made them with love.

She had a kitchen table and an old, used couch in the living room, but not much else. My cousins slept in sleeping bags on top of cardboard boxes to cushion them from the hardwood floors and from the cold. They were extremely poor but always shared whatever they had. I never got the sense that they were upset or unhappy at the excess of things others had. My cousins were always full of life and love and I enjoyed their company very much.

In fact, it is from Aunt Chris that I learned not to judge others by their possessions, not to buy into the idea that status and wealth bring happiness, and that giving people your love is the most precious of all gifts you can give or receive.

Uncle Tony and Uncle Ernie

My Uncle Tony moved back to Salt Lake City from California in the 1960s. I didn't know much about him before he came back to Utah, other than he had divorced his wife, and his two daughters stayed in California. Years later his two sons came to live with him. The boys would sometimes come over to our house with him when he'd visit. Usually, after they left, my Mom would find money missing from her purse.

Uncle Tony bought a strip bar downtown in Salt Lake City and named it the "Golden Fleece." Sometimes I would go with my mom at lunchtime to visit him. If she ever wanted to see him, that's where he'd be – at the bar. Unfortunately, he never made much money in the business. His children, who were addicted to drugs, kept helping themselves to the cash in the cash register. My cousin Georgia was his bartender and they were always fighting about the missing money from the cash register.

My mother's other brother, Ernie, moved to California before I was born, so I never really knew him growing up. The first time I met Uncle Ernie, he came to visit us on vacation. I'll never forget this short little man with silver points on the tips of his cowboy boots, wearing a black Cattleman hat and a leather vest walking up our driveway. He would stay with us for a while and then go off to visit Aunt Clee to have his fortune told. He was a simple, quiet, humble little man with a wonderful sense of humor. After he moved to Texas, he called my mother one day and told her that Texas was so flat, he could sit out on his front porch and watch his dog run away for three whole days! And that is flat – particularly for an Utahan!

He and I had a close relationship up to the end of his life. He was always fascinating and quite charming. Whenever we would talk on the phone, he would tell me about having special powers and about his conversations with aliens. He would tell me that our family was directly descended from Zeus – god of sky and thunder - and that only he and I have special powers because we won't abuse them. His father, Pappou, took him out of school after the second grade to herd sheep in the mountains. During our regular phone chats, whenever I told him something he needed to remember, he had his live-in girlfriend write it down for him.

And, ever since my mother died, he always called to say he loved me and to remind me to be a good and kind person. Sadly, the rest of my family wouldn't talk to him because of all his talk about aliens and great-grandpa Zeus. But, I would just listen. After all, who am I to judge whether he talked to aliens or not? I commune with angels sometimes!

Mom and Dad

To hear the stories told when we were young, the 'Wild West' was still alive and well in Utah in the 1950s. With 25 million acres of land, deserts, and an abundance of freshwater streams, it was perfect for raising cattle, and many large cattle ranches sprung up throughout the state. Roy Farley, was hired by the ranchers to herd cattle and sheep in the mountains of Utah. At six feet, four inches tall, with dark hair and eyes to match, he was ruggedly handsome as he sat high upon his horse. My father was a true cowboy.

When the United States entered the Korean War, my father was drafted and ultimately rose to the rank of Sergeant Major. He never spoke of the war. It was not a topic he cared to discuss. I had the distinct impression that it was a painful subject, so I never asked him about that part of his life, though there were things I heard about later.

My Mom, Tess, and dad met in Salt Lake City when she was 21 years old, he was 29. She had grown from a sheepherder's daughter to a beautiful and smart professional woman. She worked in an office downtown as a secretary. Today she'd be called an administrative assistant. After she got off from work each night, she would slowly pass the window of the bar next door, trying to catch the eye of the barkeep. He was tall and handsome with a cowboy movie star quality. She eventually did catch his eye and he'd come out onto the sidewalk to talk with her. The bartender, of course, was my dad.

As it was, my Dad might have been married, or he might have been separated. I was never really very clear on that detail. Family secrets are always the missing pieces of the story. It was clear, however, and not a secret that he had a family with children before meeting my mom. As a teenager, I once came upon my parent's marriage certificate and was surprised to learn they were married in 1957. Surprised because, born in 1956, I never knew I was probably at the wedding! Well, that kind of math, any second grader can do. It was an odd realization for me to have as a teenager; that I was a lovechild. As I recall, it didn't really make any difference to me. It was the 70s when I found out – free love and all that – and they were very much in love. And love can make a lot of things okay. Perhaps, that is one reason my dad's first family and our family got along so well. So well in fact, Dad's son (my stepbrother) married my mother's niece (my cousin, who was my Aunt Mary's daughter, the Aunt whom I never met because she was committed to a mental institution when I was just a child).

After my parent's married, my father worked for a small shop repairing typewriters and adding machines. His boss eventually got tired of running the business and decided to sell. When my mom heard that it was for sale, she saw it as a great opportunity and talked my dad into buying it. As it turned out, it was one of the best decisions they ever made together – besides me, of course. To keep costs down and help the business grow, Mom became the store's inventory control manager and secretary.

Eventually, they sold all types of office equipment; typewriters, copiers, and facsimile machines. It was a very innovative age for office equipment, electronics, and computers and my mother was a very shrewd business woman. She talked my father into selling a brand-new product to the market - the electronic cash register. Up until then, everything was manual buttons and gears. So, between his mechanical abilities and her eye for the automated future, they built a successful business, had a beautiful home, and did not want for anything.

As the years went by, Dad spent more and more time hunting and fishing, and leaving Mom to tend the business. She had a very keen business acumen and developed their product line, becoming one of the top sellers of Data Terminal Systems (the first cash registers to use UPC codes in the industry). He became pretty handy with a gun and fishing pole.

Life was good.

James 'Pappou' and Zambia 'Yiayia' and their 2-room house

Me (L) and my mother 'Tess'

My father Roy was every inch a cowboy from Utah

Uncle Ted (L) Uncle Ernie (C) and Aunt Aggie (R)

Cousins Georgia (L) Tess (R) Paul (C) Aunt Clee, and Paul's wife (R)

Uncle Ernie and a friend

Chapter 3: Growing Up in Utah

People speak sometimes about the "bestial" cruelty of man, but that is terribly unjust and offensive to beasts. No animal could ever be so cruel as a man, so artfully, so artistically cruel. – Fyodor Dostoevsky

Early Days

I was born in Richmond California, the oldest of three children. We moved to Utah when I was only two months old. Mom told me that, as a child, I hated to have anything touching my skin. She said I was constantly taking off my clothes and climbing out of my diapers. To this day, I don't like certain tactile sensations that some fabrics give me. And I especially hate wearing shoes. Come summertime, you'll find me most days in flip flops, if not bare feet. And don't get me started on bras and underwear.

My sister was born at my Aunt Aggie's house a year after I was born. She was very sweet, pretty and very feminine. I remember feeling bad for her when I got older because she had to witness me being made fun of in school. I believed she thought it was a reflection on her, and perhaps it did affect her in that way. As a lot of siblings do, she also felt that I was loved more, probably because my mom tried very hard to make me feel pretty when I was called ugly by other children. Mom's over attentiveness was purely from the compassion she had towards me for being made fun as a child. But I don't think my sister ever really knew the severity of the bullying or its effects on me.

My brother was the last in the line. I always felt a little closer to him than I did to my sister, but loved them both more than words. I remember that he was a beautiful little boy and mom was very protective of him. He was, after all, the baby of the family and her son. I realize now that I am a mom, the special relationship between mothers and sons or fathers and daughters. My dad, however, never paid much attention to him, or me for that matter. As a consequence of my father's emotional distance, I think my brother grew up trying to be accepted by everyone, and trying to gain a father's approval that was so elusive. I think that was very important to him and, like those of us who do not have a lot of guidance, we tend to think that being successful means having a lot of material things and that is what determines our self-worth.

I was five years old when I experienced my first preternatural event. I was at the playground of my Aunt Ollie's trailer park. I was running around from the seesaws to the slide when I looked up and saw a woman floating down from the sky. I wasn't afraid or even all that curious. Children often accept what they see without prejudice or denial. As I stood there looking up, she hovered above me. I don't remember what she looked like, just that she was pretty. She gave me a message. She told me that I was to do something very important. And then she was gone. I was so excited by her visit that I stopped my play and ran directly to my aunt's trailer to tell my mom, my dad, and my Aunt Ollie. They were surprised by what I told them, and brushed it off as just a child's imagination.

I did not see the sky woman after that, though I would remember her often. I wondered about her message to me and, though its meaning was beyond my understanding, felt supremely important about the idea and that she had come to *me* and gave it to *me*.

The next year I started kindergarten.

School

I believed the world was a truly beautiful place when I was a child. In my world, I was safe and loved – I loved the world and it loved me. Then I started school. That is when I met "the other world," ugly and cruel and full of children who were just like it. It seemed to me, that as soon as I entered the school grounds, they identified me as a target and started an assault by making fun of me every chance they got.

I had trouble walking as a child and Mom told me I walked like a baby elephant in those days. I also had a large, brown, splotchy birthmark that covered the right side of my face. Each day after school, they the children from the other world would chase me home, calling after me, "You're ugly. You walk funny. You're stupid. You're stupid. You're stupid. You're stupid."

They'd throw rocks, sticks, or whatever they could find lying by the side of the road. I suppose that casting out someone who looks or acts differently has been a human ritual since the dawn of man – survival of the fittest and all. But a young child doesn't know about Darwinism. They only know that they are terrified.

In some ways, more terrifying to a small child than the cruelty of children, is the cruelty of adults. Once, in school, I was asked to go to the blackboard to write the answer to a math problem. But I was so afraid of the other children I could not bring myself to move. I could not stand before my tormentors in front of the whole class. I did not refuse, per se, I just couldn't move – I sat there – frozen in my seat. It was self-preservation.

The teacher became so angry with me that she began yelling, "I told you to come up here. Now come up here!"

I could not find my voice to tell her why, in her eyes, I was being disobedient. I really did not intend to be. I was just so startled by her sudden outburst and hostility directed towards me that I did, what any terrified seven-year-old would do, I peed my pants.

How the teacher could not see the terror on my face is something I'll never understand. She could not, however, read the situation and lost her patience. She jerked me out of my seat by my arm. As I stood there, tears running down my face and urine dripping to the floor, she finally understood the scene that she had created and dismissed the class. As they filed out of the classroom, they turned - for one last look - pointed, and laughed.

After enduring years of bullying by my classmates, I began to drift into a make-believe world where I was the only inhabitant – invisible and safe. When I was in my world, the other world did not exist; it was not allowed to. My world was a magical place where I could see, but not be seen, and dreams and fantasies were my reality.

In my world, people were kind; music came from the grass and trees and carried itself through the wind. Fairies were my friends. We would build houses in the tall grass and in the trees in the back yard. I would climb up in the trees and make earrings out of the seedlings in the spring. I loved all kinds of animals and insects. I found them fascinating and would spend hours watching them. I made houses of twigs, leaves, and flowers; roads of sand and grass; buildings of bricks and rocks, and then I'd play in my very own magic land, of my very own creation.

But eventually, I'd be called back to reality and have to go back to school - to my tormentors. On a conscious level, their words worked on me. I could hear those little voices in my head saying, "You're ugly, and stupid, and you can't do that."

But at the core of me, deep inside where people truly live, I knew I was beautiful, even though the outside world did not agree. The way it saw me, the way they treated me was so foreign, so unimaginable to me that I would ask myself, *'Why do they do that? Don't they know who I am? Don't they know I am special?!"* It wasn't the boasting of a child, particularly about things they had little understanding; it was just the facts as I saw them. I knew in my heart that one day, they would see - they would see who I am and then, they'd finally understand. I guess it wasn't about that they saw or who I was, but more about who I was creating myself to be.

Sweet Sixteen and More Than Kissed

When I was sixteen, I fell in love with a boy. By the time I reached high school, the kids who made fun of me in elementary school were now jealous of me. I wasn't the homely, awkward child they used to torment and I caught the eye of more than a few football players, which, as anyone who has gone to high school knows, is money in the self-esteem bank. But I had given up on my education. I believed school was nothing more than a babysitter for parents and a way for the Government and Towns to get more tax money without paying attention to each child's special gifts.

My first love's name was Cory, and though I was not a typical girl in a lot of ways, I was a typical teenager in love. I would cut class and he would pick me up in front of Cottonwood High School on his motorcycle. We would then find secluded, secret places to be alone. And, trust me, teenagers are the best at finding them.

We had a Planned Parenthood in town, but there is a certain amount of denial that teenager's live in when they are just beginning to explore their sexuality. They know how babies are conceived but they never think it'll happen to them. Or perhaps, they find it thrilling, like playing a game of Russian roulette. Whatever it is, we did what teenagers have been doing since the dawn of man - had unprotected sex. Then, to our not exactly surprise, I got pregnant.

That was a huge wake-up call for me. I had no idea how on earth I was going to tell my parents. I was from a really good family who owned their own business and was well known in town. They would be devastated and embarrassed and, most unbearable to me, disappointed. I was not mature enough to have a child and could not bear to put my parents through such an ordeal, so my girlfriend, who was three years older than I, brought me to the Planned Parenthood. They counseled me on my options; 1) have the baby, 2) adoption, and 3) abortion. Since abortions were illegal in the state of Utah at the time, I was told I would need to go to San Francisco and have the procedure. They said they would make the arrangements with the clinic in San Francisco but that I would need to find my own way there and back.

My friends, who were my only confidants, helped me make plans to fly to San Francisco for the day and have the abortion without my parent's finding out. We planned that I would leave for school early in the morning, earlier than usual, and Karen would pick me up and drop me at the airport, and since I would be home later than usual, I would tell my parents that I was staying after for a school event.

We agreed on the plan and each of our parts, and within two weeks, I had booked a flight to San Francisco. I'd never been on a plane before and had no idea what to expect. Looking back, I am amazed at how resourceful we were. When the day came for me to take my trip, I got up as usual, preparing to go to school but was worried that my parents would somehow find out before I left. I felt dirty and stupid, just like the little children at school told me I was.

I landed in San Francisco at eight o'clock in the morning. Planned Parenthood had made arrangements for me to be picked up at the airport and taken to the hospital. As the car pulled up to the clinic (hospital? hardly!), I recognized it as an old converted convent with a large statue of the Virgin Mary. The irony of the statue greeting me as I walked past her to enter the building would have been laughable if I had not been so afraid of my circumstance and what I was about to do. Up until that point in my life, I had not been very religious but her presence was a comforting feeling that I was going to be okay.

Once inside I could smell the old plaster walls and the years of dust and mold – it was not pleasant. It was the oldest building I had ever been in and - as if my nerves weren't already frayed - it gave me the creeps. There was large desk off to the side where a woman sat with her lists and pages checking names and appointments. I was told to have a seat and someone would be right with me.

After several minutes, another woman came from behind one of the doors and called my name. I was escorted into a large room along with other young girls who were there for the same reason I was. No one smiled, except the older woman who was explaining the procedure to us. She described each step, in detail, what it would feel like, and what we could expect afterward.

After she completed her talk, she told us to take our time and to think about what we were about to do and whether we really, truly, wanted to abort or not. This was our opportunity to cut and run. I could leave and go back to Utah and have the child. Then what? As I went into the hallway and took a seat in the row of chairs outside the prep room, there was no doubt in my mind. I was not ready to be a mother.

It was an hour after lunchtime, I hadn't eaten all day and my stomach was growling. We had been told not to eat anything before the procedure, which wasn't a problem since I was too nervous to eat anyway. But now I was beginning to feel the effects of not eating – nausea, light headedness, fatigue. I just sat there, staring at all the women; some I guessed were my age and some, surprising to me, were much younger. It was all so surreal.

The woman sitting next to me was crying uncontrollably. Her boyfriend, I assumed, sat next to her and spoke to her in a low voice. I could not hear what they were saying but I did understand that she did not want to go through with the abortion. It was he who wanted her to have it and it was him insisting she do it. As bad as I felt for myself, I felt worse for her.

One by one, the chairs in the hallway emptied out. A name would be called and a girl would disappear through the door. Then, it was my turn. The room was cold. The doctor was old. The nurse was nice. And then it was over!

After the abortion, they wheeled me into a recovery room. I recognized some of the girls who had been sitting with me in the hallway. The mood in the recovery room was subdued. No one spoke. No one was happy or outwardly sad. We just drank our Sprite and ate our crackers to ease the nausea.

It was late in the afternoon before they let me leave. The car that had picked me up from the airport was now taking me back to the airport to fly home. I had a five o'clock flight and it was already four. The early May's California sun reminded me that I was a long way from home. The taxi driver regretfully told me that he doubted he could help me catch my flight on time. I began to seriously panic. I had no idea what I would do if I missed my plane. This whole perverse adventure was now traumatic.

After the car dropped me at my terminal, I ran to the airline check-in and, out of breath, laid my ticket on the counter. The attendant looked at my ticket, checked her schedule and told me I had missed my flight! And unfortunately, the next flight to Utah wasn't until the following morning and it was fully booked – there were no seats available. It was all just too much. I was physically, emotionally, and spiritually spent. I burst out in tears, sobbing uncontrollably. I had no money, didn't know anyone in California - except the other women at the clinic whom I had just shared the most intimate experience of my life with - and no way of letting my friends know that I had missed my flight. What I wouldn't have given for a cellphone!

I must have made quite an impression standing in the middle of the airport, tears streaming down my face and my shoulders heaving from stifled sobs, because a man came over and asked if he could do something to help. I could tell by his uniform that he worked at the airport, and this gave me hope. I told him that I'd just had an operation and needed to get home to Utah; that my friends were expecting me and that my parents didn't know where I was. I didn't tell him what the operation was, and now wonder if he suspected. But, it didn't matter, I needed to get home.

He listened earnestly to my trouble and then said he would see what he could do. He walked away and returned with a ticket for a flight to Utah that evening. To this day, I have no idea who he was or how he got me home that night, all that mattered was that he did. My parents never knew that I had been in California that day, or that I had had an abortion. It wasn't until years later that I finally told them.

I pretty much changed my act after that and started to study more. I got a part time job working for my parent's cash register company and learned how to program Disk Operating Systems

(DOS). I was given the responsibility of training the cashiers at all the businesses my mother sold machines to, which included grocery, retail, and liquor stores. It gave me a real sense of competence and accomplishment.

Rome Adventure Starring Jacqueline Bisset

When I was twenty-one, my mother had done so well selling cash registers she won a trip to Rome. And lucky for me, she took my sister and me with her.

It was the second time I traveled to Europe and found the old world quite different than the United States. The coliseum was full of cats, the men were lecherous, the trees were unusual, the churches absolutely breathtaking, and I embraced it all.

While my mother conducted business, my sister and I would roam around Rome, checking out the sights and browsing in the shops. We were at the Spanish Steps[iii] shopping when two men in a small Fiat drove past, noticed us, honked their horn and whistled. It was a typical, immature guy thing to do so, we did the typical mature girl thing to do and ignored them. We all went on our separate ways.

Shortly after, we stepped into a nearby shoe store. We marveled at the Italian made shoes. The smell of tanned leather hung in the air. It was a pleasant smell that encouraged us to shop. We didn't have a lot of money but it didn't matter – it was just as nice to stand there and dream. I was trying on a beautiful pair of leather boots when the same two men in the Fiat came in and started chatting up the store clerk. They were speaking in Italian so I had no idea what they were saying, and it was none of my business anyway. I saw a pair of brown leather boots that I just had to try on. The two men stood at the counter and watched as I examined the exquisite boots on my feet. The boots fit me perfectly and made me feel like a million bucks, but they were well over a hundred U.S. dollars - more than I could afford - so I knew they would not be leaving with me. Sadly, I took them off, handed them back to the store clerk, and my sister and I left.

We hadn't gotten very far when the two men came running down the sidewalk to catch up with us. Seeing them up close, not in a moving car, I could see that one man was older than the other, probably by twenty years. The older man was holding a shopping bag from the store we had just left. Holding it out to me he said, "They looked too beautiful on you for you not to have them."

I was more than surprised and a bit taken aback. I didn't know what to make of the gesture - that a man I didn't know, whom I'd never met, would buy me a pair of expensive boots. I was also leery of the gift and what it might mean in terms of "payment." I politely thanked him but told him I could not accept. He, however, would not accept my non-acceptance and proposed that I take the boots in exchange for our company over a cup of coffee. Coincidentally, or not, we stood right out front of a cafe. As the man pleaded his case, he seemed to sense our resolve waning. My sister and I conferred and agreed to join them for coffee.

Simone, the older of the two men, was a movie producer. The other, Tony, was an actor. We all spent the next hour or two drinking coffee, talking about ourselves, telling anecdotes, and laughing. They were very kind and very funny. We all had a wonderful time. When it got close to dinnertime my sister and I told them we had to get back to the hotel before my mother got worried. But, before we parted ways, Simone asked if I would join him for dinner. I told him I would need to check with my mother - she might have plans - but if she did not, I would be happy to spend the evening with him. He scribbled his address and phone number on a piece of paper and handed it to me. I took the paper and began to leave. He gently grabbed my arm and held the bag with the boots for me to take. I, once more, insisted I could not accept them. He stood firm and would not move. We remained there for a moment, until I surrendered and graciously accepted the boots.

Once I confirmed that my night was my own, I got dressed in my wrap around skirt with a birds of paradise print and my leather shoes that laced at the ankle. I grabbed a cab outside my hotel and gave the driver the address on the piece of paper. The anticipation of my evening with Simone made me nervous, in a very wonderful way. Everything seemed to be moving too slow or too fast. I wanted to be where I was going but also wanted to enjoy the moment. It was all very surreal.

After the taxi dropped me off, I climbed the stairs to the fourth floor and found Simone's flat. I knocked on the door and Simone answered. He was playing Vivaldi's 'Four Seasons' on the stereo. He led me into the living room, which was pretty insignificant in style. In fact, I thought it rather boring. I don't know what I expected but I wasn't impressed. It was nothing like how the American Hollywood types appeared to live. I settled on the couch and began flipping through the giant book laying on the coffee table. I had never seen anything like it. It had hundreds of photos – headshots – of actors. Each picture had pertinent information about the actor: name, height, weight, hair and eye color, training, experience, etc., everything a producer would need to find the right person for a part in a film. There was no denying, I was impressed and it was all very cool.

I had only been there a few minutes when his phone rang. While I perused the book, Simone went into the other room to take his call. I overheard him asking the person on the other end of the conversation to join us for dinner. When he finished, he came into the living room and asked if I would mind if a friend came along. He said his friend had just gotten into town - she was filming a movie in Rome. She was, obviously, an actress. He was being a bit sly, in retrospect, when he said I might even know who she was. Her name was Jacqueline Bisset.

"Do you know Jacqueline Bisset?" he asked.

"Of course, yes," I blurted out, "I know who she is!"

As far as America was concerned, she was only the hottest woman on the planet! I had seen *The Deep* the previous year and was enthralled by her beauty and her acting. She was currently in Rome to film *Who is Killing the Great Chefs of Europe?* with George Segal, Robert Morley, and others. The film would go on to receive a resounding two thumbs up from Siskel and Ebert upon its release.

When we pulled up to her hotel, I was in awe to see Jaqueline Bisset running down the steps to the car. She was wearing a below the knee black dress with a little fur pelt wrap around her neck. (How could I not draw a parallel between her and Cinderella leaving the ball? Though, in reality, it was I who felt like Cinderella – and her new Italian leather boots!)

When she got to the car, I got out to, free her to sit in the front seat next to Simone. After all, I was the newcomer to the party. But she insisted on sitting in the back. Simone's car was so tiny I was reminded of the clown car at the circus. Just how many movie stars and producers could we fit in here anyway? As we sped along the cobblestone streets on our way to dinner, Simone and Jaqueline chatted quickly and excitedly, trying to catch up on each other's lives. I just sat and listened. I was in awe. Here I was, a country girl from Utah, in Rome, on my way to dinner with Simone, and Jaqueline Bisset. Could my evening get any more astounding than that?

When we got to the restaurant, Simone's friend Tony was there with his girlfriend. We had a fabulous dinner in a quaint little Italian bistro in the heart of Rome. We sat huddled around the table full of empty dishes and half drank glasses of wine. I listened intently as Jacqueline told us about her family in England, her father - a doctor - whom she loved very much, and her education at the Lycée Français Charles de Gaulle in London. She spoke several languages but would often bring the conversation back to English whenever my Italian dinner companions lapsed into their native tongue.

At one point in the evening, she pulled some pennies from her purse and showed us a very cool trick, which I can't recall now, though everyone was amazed and delighted. The whole night I had feelings of belonging, but I knew I didn't. My impromptu presence in this crowd was not lost on me. These were certainly not my typical circle of friends but it didn't matter, they made me feel welcome.

I was treated to the best Italian food and wine, complimented on my green eyes, and included in their lives. But of everyone at the table, Jacqueline captivated me. She was so beautiful, so funny, and most endearing, and so considerate of me. I will always admire and respect her for that.

When we left the restaurant, and emerged on the street, there were paparazzi everywhere. The cameras' flash, like mini explosions, illuminated our faces in the city's night. I remember thinking how strange it was that they wanted our picture. I guess I felt so comfortable at dinner that I had forgotten I was with a movie star. Experienced in these types of ambushes, which is how it felt, Jacqueline grabbed my arm and told me to put my head down, not to look at the lights, and walk quickly to the car. After we climbed into the car and were on our way, it occurred to me that somewhere out there, on the paparazzi's undeveloped film, is a photo of me with Jacqueline Bisset in Rome. Wow! If I could have that picture today, it would be one of my most valued possessions. And not because it is me with a movie star but that it is me on one of the most amazing nights of my life.

After we piled into Simone's car, we all agreed that the night was young and there was still fun to be had. When we got to Simone's apartment, he opened a bottle of wine, poured everyone a glass, and put on some music. Somewhere between drinking the wine and having a great time, Simone and Jacqueline ducked out of the room.

Meanwhile, I was wedged between Tony and his girlfriend on the sofa. He had his hand on my knee and she had her hand in my hair. She would look me in the eyes and speak in Italian and Tony would translate. Sitting between them, I would look to my left, then to my right, then to the left, then to the right. She told me over and over how pretty I was, all the while stroking my hair. I felt like I was their new, favorite doll. With Simone and Jacqueline out of the room, Tony's hand on my knee and his girlfriend in my hair, I was feeling *really, really* – let me say it one more time – *really* - uncomfortable.

I was no square but I wasn't into threesomes, drugs, or any of that kind of 'fun' nonsense. I had just had a great evening in Rome with the most incredible people, but I had no idea how I would politely get myself out of this mess. Just as I was plotting my escape from Tony and his girlfriend, Jacqueline and Simone came back into the room. It was very late, three in the morning. She said she was heading back to her hotel and asked if I wanted to catch a ride with her. A huge feeling of relief washed over me as I literally jumped up from the couch and almost into her arms, gratefully accepted her offer. I often wonder if she could see how happy I was for her intervention that night.

We, Simone, Jacqueline, and I, rode back to her hotel in Simone's little car. It was late and the night was spent. He expertly navigated the narrow city avenues. When we arrived, I got out of the car, Jacqueline got out, too, and hugged me 'goodbye.' Simone tried to talk me into staying but I declined. He gave me several Lire for a taxi, told the driver my hotel's address, we said our goodbyes and I climbed into the taxicab.

As the taxi drove on, I replayed the night in my head; even today it plays like an avant garde movie. My excitement was all-consuming. I had the most amazing type of party hangover.

Slowly, the excitement began to ebb when I noticed the taxi driver staring at me through his rearview mirror. I would overt my eyes and stare out the side window and watch the Rome cityscape go whizzing by. But every time I turned to look ahead, I could see him looking back at me.

Tired and alone, I began to have some pretty dark thoughts about what could happen to a naïve American girl in Rome in the back seat of a taxi in the middle of the night. What if he pulled onto one of those dark side streets that seemed so historic and European hours before? Would he leave me dead on the roadside somewhere? With horrible scenarios floating around my brain, it occurred to me that I had left my passport at the hotel. Somehow, worst of all, my mother would never know what happened to me!

I went from thanking God for a truly marvelous evening to praying for my safe return. Somewhere between "please, please, please" and "God, God, God" the driver pulled into the back entrance of my hotel. With shaking hands, I fumbled in my purse for the money Simone had given me. Trembling and frightened, I grabbed a handful of money and literally threw it at him. Just as I reached over the front seat, he reached in back, groping for my breast. I knocked his hand away and pulled the door handle, ready to jump out. But it didn't open. The latch was broken!

Then, in that same instance, the most incredible thing happened. From nowhere, somewhere, or who knows where, a man appeared, grabbed the door handle from the outside and let me out. I tumbled out of the car, tired, confused, relieved, exhausted, and frightened. I barely acknowledged the man's presence as I ran off and through the hotel entry door.

The birthmark on my face and strange walk made me the brunt of jokes

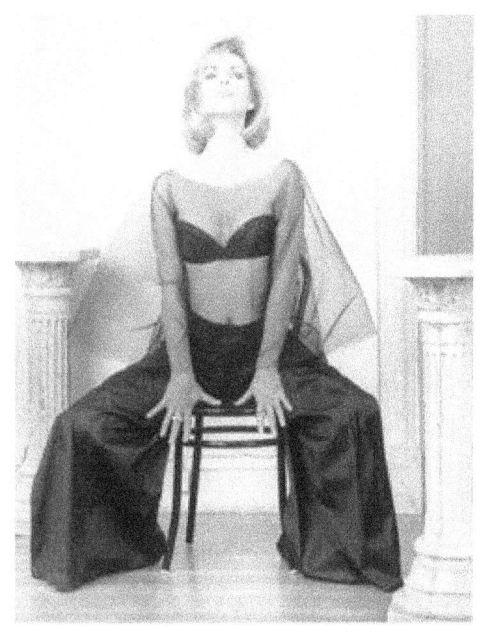

Same girl - years later when I was modeling

Chapter 4: Angels on My Shoulder

This poor man called, and the Lord heard him; He saved him out of all his troubles. The angel of the Lord encamps around those who fear him, and He delivers them. - Psalm 34:6-7

I was still sitting on my Boston Common bench, wrapped in thoughts of my childhood and reflecting on what the bag lady had said about my aunts and uncles. I was puzzling with the idea that their thoughts had, in fact, created their lives. The concept was intriguing and I believed that something more must be happening to bring about the stories of our lives.

I wondered whether this old bag lady had any connection to the old woman I saw in the dreams I had when I was very young. The dreams had the same reoccurring theme and structure. In the dream an old woman was standing by a window, seemingly, pondering the view outside. The specific window and the view from the window would often change. Sometimes it would be an old casement window in an old English cottage with multiple panes of glass. Other times it would be a plain, non-descript window from and plain non-descript room. And though the windows, as portals to the world, would change, the old woman never did. She was dressed in black, as if in mourning, and wore a black head dress, a long piece of cloth wound tightly around her almost hidden, gray hair. Sometimes I would wake from the dream to see a black figure standing at the footboard of my bed. I never really knew if I was carrying my dream into my waking life or that she was part of my life.

The physical sensations of the dream were as powerful as the imagery. I would feel within me, a magnetic pull toward her. I attributed this sense to the figure, as if she were trying to pull something from deep inside me, as if she were pulling my soul from my body. I did not find the experience frightening or feel threatened – just curious. After a short while, she would disappear! After she was gone, I was left with a feeling of relief and go back to sleep. It is not unusual for children to have reoccurring dreams that fade over time. But as I grew older, I came to understand that the old woman would be with me for the rest of my life.

Years after meeting the old woman in my dreams, I began to have surprising, out of the ordinary, other-worldly experiences. They would come out of the blue, make an everlasting impression, and be gone – leaving behind feelings of bliss, and on at least one occasion, feelings of sheer terror. They were not, by any means, the stories told by other children my age during show and tell.

One unexplainable experience came over me as I walked down a busy city street. It was just a little girl in 1963 and eight years old at the time. I was coming back from the 7-11 convenience store where I had picked-up a snack. As I passed a large empty lot near the river I used to collect pollywogs, I was overcome by an intense benevolent feeling. I could feel my whole body relaxed and I felt as though I was bathing in love. I had never known such peace and tranquility of spirit before. I was so stunned by the incredible joy I felt that I was arrested in my steps. I did not want to walk any further for fear of losing that feeling. Though wanting to stay, I knew I couldn't just stand there forever, so I eventually pulled myself back and continued on my way home. But the blessing remained with me for a several hours. I was left with the impression of a blue and white energy that surrounded me.

Though unable to understand the event at the time, I have since come to believe that I was either in the presence of an angel or touched by one. It is no small coincidence that years later on the very same street, at the very same spot I first felt that pure love The Prophet Elias Orthodox Church would be built. And years later, I would come back to that street and to the spot to be baptized in that very church.

As profoundly loved I felt after my encounter with the angel. I would later experience the antithesis of all I believed was good in God's earthly kingdom. I had, what can only be described as a preview of things to come for some poor souls during a 7th grade art class. Sitting at my easel, I was suddenly overcome by a feeling of pure dread, of something that felt as black and cold as the isolation of outer space, and pure evil. It surrounded me for a few moments and then was gone. Though the feeling had come and gone, a nagging anxiety followed me throughout the school day. I told my only friend Leah about it. She lived behind me and I would sometimes let her into my make-believe world. We were inseparable, so much so that the school tried to separate us. Who knows why? We never got into trouble; we just always wanted to be near one another. In some way, I believed she felt sorry for me being made fun of so much in school.

When the weekend came, Leah invited me to sleep at her house. It was not the first time I had slept over so I was pretty comfortable with the layout of her home, her bedroom and, more importantly, where the bathroom was.

We had stayed up late watching television, eating snacks, drinking soda, and talking about school, boys, and the like. Eventually we dozed off and fell asleep. I have no idea how long I'd been sleeping when I woke, feeling the urge to go. Groggy with a sleepover hangover, I climbed out of bed and started to make my way to the bathroom. I could feel the plush piled carpet on my bare feet and hear the sound of my soles dragging along it. As I rubbed the sleep from my eyes, I looked down to see that I was standing on a carpet of worms. Hundreds and thousands of them twisted and squirmed under foot and all around me. I did not fully comprehend what was happening. I ran over to the bed where Leah lay sleeping. I shook her shoulder urgently, and her head wobbled back and forth, but she did not wake.

As I looked around the room trying to make sense of this place, demons materialized all around me. I was sucked down into a dark evil vortex. If this was our fate, I prayed for God to take me and not Leah. At the time it seemed the right thing to do because I loved her so much. Looking back, I am a bit surprised at my selfless love in such terror.

I ran over to the basement stairs trying to get away from them. At the bottom of the stairs I saw a pit of dead bodies – hundreds, thousands, tens of thousands, hundreds of thousands - and people stepping on the dead, screaming and waving their hands in the air, as if looking for someone to help them get out.

Years later I would see the same scenes depicted on the ceilings of cathedrals and in paintings of Europe. But for now, I was surrounded by ghastly demons torturing, and tearing at my body. I remember being aware that there were others trapped in this place with me. I could not see them or them me but we had an awareness of each other's presence. We were unable to communicate. There was like a veil of silence that surrounded us but we were merely trapped together. I found myself running from room to room in my girlfriend's house trying to wake someone.

But it was of no use. I was in a different world within that room; as if on a different plane or in another dimension. As I witnessed this ungodly scene, I was consumed by a feeling of total disconnection from life. It was as if the world had ended and I was just stuck in that frame of reference for all eternity. For the first time in my life I felt as though there was no meaning. There was only a void left by nothingness and fear - absolute and total fear. I was locked inside a thought that I couldn't change. In my heart and soul, I knew that what I was experiencing and where I was, was Hell.

With this realization I began sweating and crying out for God to help me, begging Him to save me. Then, within my mind's eye, I had a vision of kneeling in Jesus' palm, and He was crying. At that moment, I felt that I had been in Hell for quite some time before the Savior came for me. My entire life, as young as I was, was played out before me; the hospital where I was born; the doctors and nurses who helped deliver me; my horrible elementary school days; my foot deformity and my facial birthmark, the catcalls from the other kids; all the events in my life leading up until that moment. I felt so sorry for the way I had been, for all the stupid things I had done. I then understood how much I had been given and how I had neglected the beauty of the world.

After my life was revealed, I no longer stood in Jesus' palm and I was no longer in the other pit of Hell. It was 2 AM and I wanted to go home. Still in my pajamas and barefooted, I left my friend's house and ran down the darkened street to my house. When I got home, no one was there. My parents and siblings had gone out of town for my parent's anniversary. Frightened and alone, I phoned the police and told them I needed help. It was Friday, September 13th and the worst night of my life!

I felt a terror that day that I had never experienced before, or since. After my view of the chilling abyss, I felt an enormous compassion for anyone who might be sent there, which included the worst of mankind such as serial killers, or even a Hitler. It was soul crushing and horrifying! When I look back on it, I would describe it as the Hell found in the Bible. I cannot, and will not ever deny His existence—as I cannot—for he saved me at one of the darkest hours of my life.

I am not sure that I believe in the Hell and damnation taught in Catechism. But I do know that the mind is capable of conjuring it from our thoughts and feelings, and bringing into our consciousness. That is why I believe we should try to find peace in our lives and practice *making it a state of mind every day, especially before the last hour of our death.*

When I began exploring my spirituality I began researching the Mysteries[iv]. In them I found confirmation that there is a dark side to this world. I believe I had always known that the magical world of my childhood had an 'evil twin,' but never had it been so clear to me before experiencing the Mysteries. And though my aunt was a psychic and card reader, I now saw that if someone was practicing the art of card reading, they had better damn well know what they were doing!

Chapter 5: Life as a Single Mother

Mind is indeed the Builder . . . what is held in the act of mental vision becomes a reality in the material experience. We are gradually built to that image created within our own mental being. - Edgar Cayce

The Wish List – Education and Edification

When I was young, I dreamt of going to college, getting an education and a degree. One class I really enjoyed in school was biology. The human brain, how it worked, and why things happen the way they do fascinated me. I would often fantasize about becoming a neurologist. And, despite all I had endured and after Russell died, I eventually found my way to college.

In the spring of 1983, I enrolled in English Literature 101 at the University of Utah. It was not neurology but it was a start – I was officially a college student, which sounded grand indeed.

One of my first classroom assignments was to create a wish list. I thought, 'This'll be easy, who doesn't have a wish or two beating in their heart?' The professor, Dr. Lori Steinberg[v] gave us specific instructions for our assignment. First, we were to be very clear and concise about are wishes. They had to be obtainable - based in reality I think she meant. Secondly, we were to post our list in plain sight so that we would see it and could concentrate on it, daily. We had to make the wish list one of the thoughts we had each day. "If you follow these steps," she told us, "at some point in your life, you will receive everything on your list." I thought to myself, 'uh-huh, I *wish* it was that easy!'

An alternative to the list was a photo of a desired object – again, based in reality and not from the next galaxy over.

She told us of a letter she received from a former student of hers who had been given the same assignment. Instead of writing a list, he used the image of a coveted car from the cover of a magazine. He took the page showcasing a shiny, new red Ferrari and stuck it on his bathroom mirror. Every morning as he shaved and brushed his teeth, his car smiled back at him from the mirror.

Sometime after attending her course, he dropped out of school and went to work as an auto mechanic at a local gas station. One day, while at work, a tow truck with a long flatbed stopped at the pumps to gas up. Looking out the garage door he nearly dropped his tools. Sitting atop the bed of the truck was a beautiful red Ferrari with some pretty extensive damage. It had been in a wreck and the truck was hauling it off to the junkyard. He decided right then that he wanted that car. After wrangling and negotiating with the tow truck driver and wrangling and negotiating with the junkyard, he bought the car – the red Ferrari was his! He spent the next several years repairing the damage, working on the engine and replacing parts in order to bring it back to its pre-collision glory.

But she saved the most interesting part of the story for last. After he purchased the car he began doing research for the repairs, and that is when he found out that the car he had bought was, in fact, the very same year, make and model of the car from the magazine cover! Well, of course, after hearing that I was all over this new homework assignment!

Sitting in that literature class I thought to myself that if all this 'wish list' stuff was really true, I had better be careful. So, after considerable thought I came up with my list:

1. To have a home in the Harvard area
2. To be a good mother and raise healthy children -- physically and emotionally.
3. To get closer to God.
4. To someday live on or near the water.
5. To write a bestselling book.
6. To meet and marry a warm, loving man.
7. To become financially stable.

I spent a year and a half enrolled at the University of Utah but it didn't take long before I realized I could not pursue a doctorate degree and still be the parent I wanted to be, which was both mother and father to my little boy. So, I did what I felt I had to do; I gave up on that dream, left school, and got jobs as a secretary, a model, and a waitress in order to pay the bills.

But the exercise of the wish list never was far from my mind. It went with me, through all my travels. And as the years went by, I slowly began to see some of these things materialize. Maybe I was the creator of my destiny after all.

The Farmhouse

Growing up, I used to peer over the fence between our house and a one-acre property next door to see the pretty horses our neighbors owned. I would watch the horses roamed around the land for hours. They would eat at the plush green meadow grass and circle the little, tiny yellow house made from cinderblock and wood. I saw their homestead as a magical place with a large weeping willow and many elms trees. I always wondered what was in the old barn in the back of the property.

An elderly couple had lived there for years. Before the old man retired, he worked for the Bureau of Indian Affairs and spent a lot of time on the reservation with the Ute Indians. He was an interesting fellow to listen to when he would chitchat with my mother or father over the property line.

Behind the house was a shed he'd converted into his own home away from home. He would go out there to smoke cigarettes and drink vodka because his wife would not allow it in their house. He made it look quite rustic with a stone fireplace made of creek-bed rocks, old broken antique bottles, and dinosaur fossils. It was certainly what we would call a "man cave" today.

Shortly after his wife died, he put the home on the market. My mother, always looking for a good investment, went over to discuss selling it to her. He said he would sell it to her provided she promised to never raze it to construct a housing development. My mother, who wasn't in the construction business anyway, agreed and the sale was made.

Sadly, a month after he moved out of the house, we learned he had committed suicide. We assumed he missed his wife so much that he could not find a reason to go on living.

Although it was a farmhouse and sat back from the road, it was on very busy and, sometimes, noisy street. In the evenings, when I went to bed, I would pretend the sound of the cars roaring by were actually undulating ocean waves. The ebb and flow of the engine and road noise from a car approaching, then, moving away, gave me the sensation of being on the beach, the waves rising and rolling in, then crashing on land and receding back to the sea. If I maintained this image in my mind's eye, I would put myself to sleep every night under the stars, in the sand with the ocean at my command. I suppose I could have bought a tape of meditation nature sounds but I enjoyed creating my world near the water. It was mine whenever I needed it.

I didn't know how much I would need it until Christopher began having epileptic seizures. He was about two years old and it was dinner time. I was in the kitchen and Christopher was in the living room playing on the floor. I looked around the corner to check on him and saw him lying on the floor in the midst of a convulsion. His eyes were rolled back in his head and he was choking and drooling. I picked him up, trying to understand what was happening. He wretched and twisted in my arms, I let out a scream and ran to the phone. I carefully laid him down on the floor so he would not twist himself out of my arms and called 911.

The dispatcher heard the frantic fear in my voice and tried to calm me down. She realized I was describing a seizure and calmly told me that help was on the way. She kept talking to me, asking me questions, looking for details about what was happening and, all the while, reassuring me that he would be okay.

The paramedics arrived within minutes. And while they cared for Christopher and got him ready to go to the hospital, they, too, assured me he would be okay.

But the whole heart-pounding scene was more than I could stand. It pushed me over the edge. I went into the bathroom and closed the door. I sat on the closed toilet lid and, for the first and only time in my life, I screamed at God - this all-encompassing life force, this omnipotent being. *"God," I yelled, "you can do whatever you want to me! But you leave my son the FUCK alone!"* I was not only surprised that I used the "f" word, which isn't part of my vocabulary, but I was shocked that I had used it in the same sentence as God.

After the hospital released Christopher, I made an appointment with his pediatrician. The pediatrician examined him and ordered some tests. When the test results came back, the doctor called to tell me that they were inconclusive. He reassured me that he did not have a brain tumor – thank God – and did not have any brain damage. In summation, he had no idea why Christopher was having the fits.

While the knowledge that he did not have a tumor or brain damage was heartening, it was short lived as the seizures continued and we found ourselves at the Emergency Room on a weekly basis. The doctors poked, prodded, tested, examined, and puzzled over Christopher and his condition. And after a couple weeks, and many tests later, they came back to me with the clinically exhaustive analysis -- "He's an enigma." They could not find a clinical foundation for the grand mal seizures he'd was experiencing.

With that understanding, we agreed to find a medication that would control the seizures, at the very least. So, with that strategy, we tried a medication called Phenobarbital, but it caused him to break into a rash and run a fever. After several other unacceptable medications, we found one that his little body could tolerate. The trade off, however, between the terrifying spasms that wracked his body and the medication to control them was that it was a high-risk drug that killed antibodies, antibodies his body needed to fight off disease and infection. It felt as though I was choosing between two evils, and I was.

Each week I would take him to the hospital to have his blood drawn so they could monitor his red blood cell count. Each week I would wait for the call from his doctor, waiting to hear the numbers – the score – on how he was this week. Your children are always on you mind, anyway, but this added a new layer of worry to his condition. And the fact that all the decisions about this little boy's life lay squarely in my hands alone was unbearably stressful. Up this point, many things in life had brought me to my knees, and this was certainly one of them.

The Monk and the Miraculous

The medication and the monitoring had gone on for a year or more when I heard about a monk who lived in an old monastery in New England, quite distant from Utah, and who, it was said, had powerful prayers that could heal. I had heard from many people of his healing prayers so I had no reason to doubt that it was possible and, truthfully, never really gave it much thought. I suppose like many people I believed in traditional medicine, like going to the doctor whenever something ailed you. Now, however, in the case of my son, traditional medicine was letting me down and I was desperate. I was a mother willing to do whatever it took to help her son, including flying half-way across the United States to see a religious healer if that's what it took. So, I got his phone number and made the call.

When the Monk answered the phone, I felt a relief wash over me. I don't know if it was his soothing voice or that I now had someone who might actually be able to help me, someone with whom to share my struggle. I wanted to be clear with him from the beginning. I told him I did not practice his religion but was praying he could help, and that I'd heard he could cure my son.

"I can't cure your son. Only God heals," he replied. "But I will read prayers over him."

A week later I was driving down a long, beautiful, tree-lined driveway with my son Christopher in the backseat, on my way to a large, Scottish style manor in Brookline, Massachusetts. On the plane ride from Utah, I told Christopher we were going to a place that was very special, that it would be nothing like a hospital or a doctor's office and this would be the day his sickness would go away. I encouraged him to be brave because when we left, he would be all better.

I believed everything I told Christopher with all my heart and I wanted him to believe it too. I know there is power in believing, whether it is something good or bad, going back to 'Mind is the builder.'

I was in awe of the beautifully manicured grounds and well-cared for brick mansion as I came up the drive. Under a recessed archway, a set of large wood-carved, antique doors greeted us. Anticipating our arrival, the monk opened the door to the entrance.

"Hi Pam, I'm Father Isaac," he said and shook my hand.

He then introduced himself to Christopher. He was very kind, and the epitome of an elderly monk with a full white beard and a long black robe. Standing in the vestibule of the imposing house, I was overcome by the aroma of burning incense and the larger than life icons of Jesus, Mary, and the Holy Saints that greeted us. Golden halos and merciful faces looked down on me and my son as if in reassurance – reassurance that I was in good hands. I felt nervous, awestruck, and at peace.

Father Isaac led us down the hall to the chapel. The chapel was a narrow room with incredibly high, arched ceilings. At the altar, I saw two pendants of light illuminated images of Jesus Christ, the Virgin Mary, and other saints. They all looked back at me.

Christopher, my beautiful little boy, walked hand-in-hand with Father Isaac to a corner at the head of the chapel. They stood next to the large antique icon of the Virgin Mary and a large golden candelabrum, beneath leaded glass windows. I stood off to the other corner of the room. I watched as this Holy Man placed his prayer vestment over the head of my son and rested his hand there. He closed his eyes and began praying quietly over my son. Christopher remained still and quiet. After few minutes, in the still and the quiet of the chapel, Father Isaac took in a deep breath and my son let out a giggle. At that moment, I felt my heart grow lighter and I knew - *I knew* - that Christopher was better; that all I had told him on the plane had come true - *he was healed.*

After the healing in the chapel, Father Isaac escorted us back to the beautiful, carved doors in the vestibule. I could not help but feel the difference in the day and in my heart from when I first walked through them just a couple hours before. I thanked the him and asked him what I owed. He said I owed nothing and refused to take any money. Christopher held my hand as we walked to the car and I told him that he was all better – just as I had promised. At the age of five I don't think he quite understood what I meant or how important it was to me. That very same day, I began to slowly decrease his prescribed dose and wean him off his seizure medication. Three months later he was medicine – and more importantly – seizure free.

Sometime afterward, I received a call from Christopher's pediatrician. I had not been taking him to the lab to have his red blood cell count monitored and he wanted to know why. I related the whole story to him about the monk, the monastery, and the healing. And I am sure he thought me quite fanatical, insane, or both. He asked me to bring Christopher for a brain scan – again – which I did. He called a few days later with the test results. He said there was no indication of seizure activity and, given my report of peace and quiet, he saw no reason to keep him on anti-seizure medication. He told me to thank God and dismissed Christopher as his patient, with a clean bill of health. There is no better feeling a mother can have than to know that their children are happy and healthy. And though my son has experienced other trials in his life, the curse of a lifetime of seizures is not one of them.

After Christopher's healing, life settled into our usual routine, but the experience I had in Boston was never far from my mind. Then one day, my girlfriend B.J. came over to the farm for her usual morning coffee visit. She had been reading *Cosmopolitan* magazine – and in this particular issue was an article about Boston, Massachusetts, "the greatest city in America." I had an affinity to the old city, particularly after my visit to the monastery where Christopher was healed and it was, after all, on my wish list.

So, after a short scouting trip to the area, I made a bold and scary decision. I packed up all my belongings, all my hopes and dreams, took my young son and moved to Massachusetts. Once there I found an apartment in Newton Lower Falls, a mere ten-minute drive to Harvard.

I was tired of tragedies and all the evil I saw in the world, and fatigued by the spiritual and emotional pain in my own life. So, when I got to Boston I joined the Greek Orthodox Church, the church of the man who given me so much comfort and solace when my son was ill. I felt as though it was, once again, coming to my rescue. I wanted to go into a life of prayer, to help myself and to help others. This world I had come to know was so different than what I had imagined when I was four. I wanted to leave the outside world for the inside world the Church could offer.

One of the first things I needed to do to become part of the Church community was to get a spiritual father. I went to see a lovely priest named Father Christos. He was very kind and helped initiate me into the Church and her dogmas. At the first meeting, he gave me a little booklet to read about a Russian woman named Saint Xenia. It was a story about a homeless clairvoyant. [vi] At the end of the reading, it said she asked people to pray for her so, I began praying for her. It wasn't until years later, I found out that *I was supposed to be praying to her to help me*, not the other way around. I thought, oh well, everyone needs a little prayer help now and then, even saints.

After reading the book he had given me about Saint Xenia, I confided in Father Christos that I had had vivid dreams and clairvoyant experiences as a child and as an adult. Father Christos told me that only saints and very great ascetics[vii] possessed these powers and that whatever I was experiencing had to be something else. But I knew that whatever happened at those times was not of my own doing.

One such experience was a dream of a woman lying down, face upward, as if asleep. The woman did not seem young or old, she was rather ageless. I watched as she slowly began to rise above her resting place, ascending toward the heavens. As she rose higher, she became upright and continued to ascend. As she floated skyward, she gracefully transformed into different types of angels, rising higher and higher, until she metamorphosed into a beautiful archangel. When I awoke I was full of awe and at peace. I called my Mom the next day to tell her about my dream. She told me that my Aunt Chris, who had been living at Mom's house while dying of pancreatic cancer, had passed away the night before. It gave me great comfort to know that my aunt was in heaven and receiving her just reward because she had suffered so greatly during her life on earth.

Another unexplainable event happened when I was in my twenties and dating a really nice guy named David. He had invited me over to his place for a relaxing evening of listening to music, drinking wine, and eating cheese and grapes. I can still hear the music in my ears when I think of my evening with him. It was the *Concierto de Aranjuez – Adagio* a truly beautiful piece by Joaquin Rodrigo. I sat on the couch listening to the melody. He stood by the window looking out – seemingly transfixed by the ethereal notes. He motioned for me to come over to the window as he pointed to something in the yard. I got up and joined him and looked to see what he was pointing to. At the window I saw that I wasn't in Utah anymore. I was no longer wearing the jeans and button up shirt I had dressed in. I now wore a long dress of thick velvet-like material with a high, white collar. I seemed to have been mystically transported to a medieval time. The walls were no longer plain plaster and paint but were now made of stacked stone. The window we stood at was just an open port with no glass. It looked down onto a grass field where a long line of soldiers in a column formation marched down a long dirt road and over the top of a neighboring hill. I knew they were off to war and that I was saying goodbye to David, who was going to join them. It only lasted a moment, but the details and the emotions of the vision were vividly clear and felt absolutely real.

I now stood at the window with David, in his home, stunned. I looked at him and said, "Wow, I just had a weird experience."

He met my glaze and I could see he was a bit perplexed too. He said, "So did I."

"What was yours?" I asked.

He described standing in a room with stone walls, at a glassless window with me by his side in a long dress with a white collar. From there the vision remained the same – the view out the window, the long line of solders marching onward, and the knowledge they were off to war.

Did we have wine? Yes, we did. Were there drugs involved? Absolutely not!

I had never had anyone join me in a vison and I never really understood why we experienced it together. Perhaps it was a view of what was, or might have been in another lifetime.

But my all-time favorite premonition came many years later when I had been given the great fortune of traveling to Jerusalem - the Holy Land, with the monks, nuns, and a group of parishioners from my new Church. I was profoundly inspired as I walked the roads that Jesus walked and be in the very places I read about in the Bible. I was totally mesmerized by the Holy Land and my senses worked overtime trying to absorb everything from this divine place. It turned out to be a profound historical experience as well as a spiritual journey.

One of the stops on the tour in Jerusalem was the Church of the Holy Sepulcher. Outside the narrow entrance stood a monk, seemingly a guard of sorts, and a nun. We each, in turn, had to crouch low to enter the tomb where Jesus Christ was placed after dying on the cross. The tomb was very small inside but I still managed to I kneel. I rested my head on the tomb wall and asked God to watch over my sons and to make me a better person. When I had finished my prayer, I got up off my knees and exited through the narrow tomb entrance. As I emerged into the light of day, I looked down and noticed a prayer rope on the ground near the door to the tomb. I picked it up and felt the braided material. It was a well-used prayer rope, smooth and worn from years and years of prayer. I thought it most surely belonged to the nun who had been standing with the monk when I entered, so I asked him, "Did you see that nun who was here?"

He looked at me earnestly and said, "What nun?"

"The nun who was standing next to you," I told him, feeling as though I didn't really need to explain.

"There was no nun here," he replied.

"Yes, there was," I insisted, holding out the rope for him to see, "She probably dropped her prayer rope."

The puzzled monk paused and said, "Consider it a gift from God."

Though I accepted the unexplainable, other worldly events as part of my life, their meaning remained a mystery to me. And I believed the Church was where I would find some answers. But first I needed someone who would not discount my experiences, as Father Christos had done, so I went to see Father Isaac. He told me to tell him whenever these occurrences happened and he would help discern them. I was relieved and happy that I had finally found someone who would listen and help. From that point on, Father Isaac became my trusted Spiritual Father.

After that, I began a ferocious diet of reading. I spent hours on spiritual readings, gathering whatever information I could about the great ascetics[viii] and saints. I read about their lives and began emulating their rites and rituals. I connected everything I was learning about metaphysics and physics, to spirituality and I saw links between them all; the instruments they used, the incense, the tones of prayer, and the common drive to search. I was more and more drawn to "New Age" reading material. I had created a library full of books from Marianne Williamson, Shakti Gawain, Herman Hesse, and books on Buddhism, Hinduism - and any *ism* I could find. I was frantically searching for truth. I attended different denominations and churches in the Boston area as well. I wanted to find one that "fit." I was determined to find God. I had become a religious zealot and was sure that the closer I came to finding grace, the stronger I would be and that I could help, what I was sure, was a sick world, or as I had come to learn - a world asleep. By God, I thought, I was going to find out how to heal it! I felt so blessed, that with my new found calling, I set my course and committed to raising my sons, and then someday maybe, becoming a nun.

However, I learned quickly, as I had when I went back to school, that raising a child (especially by yourself) required an income, patience, strength, and many other things that do not leave much time for study.

So, putting my self-education on hold, off to work I went.

Father Isaac and Christopher after our first to visit the Monastery

Chapter 6: A New Life in Boston

Yeah, down by the river,
Down by the banks of the river Charles,
(Aw, that's what's happenin' baby)
That's where you'll find me,
Along with lovers, muggers, and thieves
(Aw, but they're cool people)
Well I love that dirty water,
Oh, Boston, you're my home

- *"Dirty Water" © 1966 The Stqndells*

The Original Boston Rascal

After settling into my new life, I found I had already obtained a few things on my wish list. I was living in the Harvard area, I did everything I knew to be a good mother, and I was working very hard to become financially stable. I was out to make it on my own - without the help of a man!

I found a job as a legal secretary in a law firm on Beacon Street, across from the beautiful Boston Commons. On warm, sunny days I would leave my desk and the business offices to take a walk on the Commons and eat my lunch. I loved sitting in the sunshine, feeding the birds my leftover bread, and watching people rushing by or just enjoying the world, like me. I was very happy-go-lucky and friendly to my fellow Commoners, which was a disposition that bothered one of the partners at the firm. He was 40 years my senior and appointed himself my Irish stepfather.

His name was John Cremens; as charming, old, roly-poly Boston Irishman, if I ever there was one. He fit the part of the quintessential Irish Boston Pol from central casting with his round, red face and carefully coiffured Donald Trump comb-over.

He would often say in his Boston Irish accent, "Jeeesuss Christ, don't be smilin' at strangers when you go out for lunch. You don't know any of these people or who might follow a pretty gurl like you home!"

Cremens was very well-connected politically. I'd often see him through the open office door, sitting at his large antique desk, the bookcase behind him just a wall of law books, negotiating some deal or another on the telephone. He was exceptionally proud to be the Captain Commander in the Massachusetts Ancient and Honorable Artillery Company (AHAC), which was established in 1638 by the King of England. The AHAC's most notable and distinguished members were James Monroe, Chester Arthur, Calvin Coolidge, and John F Kennedy. Cremens would brag to anyone who would listen about how he could be buried with history's notables such as Samuel Adams, John Hancock, and Robert Treat Paine in the 'old Granary Burial Ground.' Just the thought of it, being buried in such an old, decrepit cemetery frightened me. Who knew what spirits would creep out if they ever dug up that old place to make room for another body?!

One of my favorite stories told by John was about how he came to own an old Rolls Royce, which he drove to work and around town. As the story goes, Queen Elizabeth came to Boston on the QEII during the country's bicentennial celebrations in 1976. As the Captain Commanding of the AHAC, he was asked to be part of the welcoming committee at the old State House, along with Mayor Kevin White and Massachusetts Governor Michael Dukakis. During the ceremonies, he was to present her with an antique silver bowl crafted by Paul Revere, bow graciously, and move along the reception line. But, playing the part of the Irish rogue, when he was standing before her, bowl in hand, he took the opportunity to tell the Queen that there were new divorce laws in the United States and that she should get rid of Prince Phillip and run away with him that very night. Queen Elizabeth accepted the bowl and chuckled. Prince Phillip rolled his eyes. Mayor White turned...well...white and just about fainted and Governor Dukakis laughed. To Cremens' surprise, he was invited to tea on the Royal Yacht HMY BRITANNIA the very next day. He said he had a grand time and made the entire royal party laugh. And so, it was some years later that he received a phone call from the manager of the Boston shipyard informing him that his Rolls Royce had arrived from Bermuda. He said he never ordered anything, let alone a Rolls Royce! But he said he suspected who it was from. He always insisted that the car had belonged to Princess

Margaret for her use while she was in Bermuda and that it had been a gift from the Queen of England!

Do I believe it? Knowing John Cremens – absolutely! There's only so much blarney you can get from an Irishman!

A Friend and a Father

It was John who introduced me to Jimmy, insisting that I make a date with him. I wasn't much interested in romance at the time, I was focused on establishing myself in Boston and getting Christopher and I settled into our new life. But John pushed and prodded and I finally relented. I agreed to one date.

Jimmy was much older than I by almost 30 years. I thought lunch would be a nice change from the school events with my young son, which had become my only social life.

I wasn't surprised to find that Jimmy was as charming as his buddy John Cremens. They both had those cute Boston accents and told stories with big giant smiles. They could draw you into any story about anything as if you were being told the secrets of the universe. He, an Irishman and Navy veteran like Cremens, had put himself through law school on the GI Bill after serving in the Korean War. In the 1960s he had been an advance man for President Kennedy and always referred to him as Jack. And though I was never impressed by name dropping, I must confess to being a little impressed that I had met someone who called President Kennedy by his nickname.

Jimmy was living on Cape Cod when we started dating and had just finished co-writing *Senatorial Privilege* with Leo Demore. The book is an account of the 1969 Chappaquiddick tragedy involving Ted Kennedy and Mary Jo Kopechne. It was a topic he knew quite well since he had been friends with the Kennedy brothers – Ted and Bobby – and served as the Assistant District Attorney of Massachusetts when Teddy drove off the old wooden bridge on Chappaquiddick Island after leaving that fateful party.

After we had been dating a while, he confided that he, too, was supposed to be at the party that night. But something came up at the last minute, so he couldn't attend. During the evening, he received a phone call from a friend in the police department and was told what had happened.

He was very good to me and kind to my son, Christopher. I had not, up to that point in my life, had a relationship with a man who actually liked and respected me (the blessed monk not included). It was very intoxicating to be with someone who looked at me with love and kindness – not enmity and anger.

He was very interested in my life and my ideas for improving the public schools in Boston, so he arranged for me to meet with Jon Silber, the President of Boston University, and Bob Antonucci, the Superintendent of Boston Public Schools. I had developed a proposal to get a program introduced into the school system to help children with self-esteem issues. I understood, from my own childhood experience, that if things were going on at home, it would have an emotional and sometimes physical effect on him or her at school. Though we, of the baby boom generation, watched TV families like *Ozzie and Harriet*, *The Donna Reed Show*, and *Father Knows Best*, no one I knew grew up in that idealized world. And the messiness of real family life could make it very difficult to learn or to concentrate when your mind was full of events at home.

In my efforts to be a supportive parent, I purchased whatever I could get my hands on to bolster Chris' emotional security; books, tapes and anything that I thought would support him and give him a sense of just how special he was. One set of tapes was chock full of songs children could sing to themselves and others about how unique they were. They were from the "Bright Beginnings" program developed by someone in Salt Lake City.

For my school program, I wanted to add a component where middle school children would get together in groups, either inside or outside the school, to have conversations about what was going on in their lives, with parental permission and adult supervision, of course. Along with the songs, I had compiled a series of home and school assignments that would give them an opportunity to learn about and research the consequences of bullying and other troubling issues for children. Then after the assignments were completed, they would be able to express their thoughts and experiences in a safe, supportive environment. In the end, my proposal got rave reviews but no funding - like many other progressive programs. We always seem to, as a society, have wonderful ideas but shortage of cash. Or is it will?

I learned from Jimmy that I was valuable and smart, and began to develop a confidence I never had before. I loved him as a person but he was so much older than I was, and it showed in our individual interests. We just had too many differences, like our musical tastes. He did the jitterbug, and you just can't do the jitterbug to techno or alternative rock. I was bored to death with politics. He was consumed by it. He had no energy for going out and doing things. I was full of energy. And the list went on and on. So, to say the least, I was devastated to find out that I was pregnant at the exact time I was ready to end the romantic relationship and just be friends.

I decided to tell Jimmy at his 60th birthday party. I really didn't know what to expect or how he was going to take the news. Admittedly, I joked that he was going to have a heart attack but never dreamt – or intended - that he would actually have heart attack – literally – a heart attack!

After the birthday party on the Cape, I drove back to my home in Newton. I had no sooner come in the door when I got a phone call from one of his children. Jimmy was admitted to the hospital for, presumably, a heart attack. I got in my car and rushed to the hospital. I did not know what to expect once I got there. They had taken Jimmy to the cardiac care unit. When I came around the corner and saw him hooked up to all the monitors with their squiggly lines and soft interrupting beeps, it made my own heart sink. I went to his bedside and took his hand so that he would know I was with him. We remained there awhile, just being together.

Whether he had a near death experience or not, I don't know, but he later told me he saw Chris and me standing in the doorway with a little boy, and the little boy told him that he was coming to be there for Chris. He said he knew then that he had to come back from the afterlife for that boy. In February of 1990 I gave birth to Jonathan named for our dear friend John Cremens.

After Jimmy was released from the hospital, we continued our relationship and celebrated the prospect of raising our child together. But there was something missing. He felt it and so did I. We were not on the same wavelength and it created, as best I can describe it, a dissonance. He was from one generation and I was from another. We often had to contextualize our experiences. We weren't intuitive with each other – not the way couples should be. At times, we could have been speaking two different languages. I did not believe that being with someone should ever be that hard. In the end, our differences became bigger than our love for each other. We parted ways amicably before I gave birth, but promised we would be friends forever and raise the child together – which we have and we do.

With Jimmy no longer a part of my daily life, I decided to gather my son, Christopher, pack up my things and return to my family in Salt Lake City to have my baby.

If Only

Shortly after Jonathan was born, I returned to Boston, the city I had come to love and consider my real home. With now two kids in tow, I set about rebuilding my east coast life.

I returned to work, but it was very hard leaving the boys with babysitters so, I took temporary assignments through a placement firm where I could pick and choose weekly assignments that fit my schedule and needs. I also did some modeling part-time which was decent pay when I could get it. Most of the money I earned went to paying someone else to babysit the children, which often happens when you are a single mother and the only breadwinner. One thing I was proud of during those difficult times was that I never needed to apply for welfare. After seeing how my mother's siblings lived, without money or ambition, I swore I would not bring my children up that way. The only public assistance I accepted was on behalf of my children. I did apply for school lunch aid so they were well fed and there was one less thing for me to do while getting all out the door in the morning.

One of my temporary job assignments was as a receptionist at a large law firm. The business model of employing people without actually employing people was new at the time. But I was happy to have the work. Being the newbie in the office, I had not made a lot of work friends, yet. I would often sit at my desk to eat a sandwich and read a book during my lunch hour. One afternoon, my head buried in a book and my half-eaten sandwich sitting on my desk waiting for another bite, one of the firm's young attorneys walked by.

Then he walked by again, and again, and again. He never said anything, or even slowed his pace but I knew he was on a self-subscribed reconnaissance mission - he was checking me out. And though I was intently absorbed in reading my book, I did happen to notice that he had delicately chiseled features, dark brown hair, and sweet caramel colored skin with gorgeous cerulean blue eyes.

This dance went on for weeks until he actually stopped at my desk and introduced himself. He extended his hand and I shook it. "Don't shake my hand weakly; it shows you can be taken advantage of," he said as he as he extended this large, beautiful hand to me again. And though, with anyone else I might have taken offense, in all truthfulness, it was a pleasure to hold his hand in mine again, so I shook it. To which he replied, "Work on it."

With the handshaking lesson over, our conversation turned to the book I had been reading. I told him that it was a biography about the Grand Duchess Elizabeth; granddaughter of Queen Victoria of England and the sister of Alexandra, the wife of Czar Nickolas of Russia. He seemed interested in the subject and took the book from my hands. He flipped through a few pages – as if looking for pictures – and told me that his family was from a country near Russia. "I'm Latvian," he said and left.

After our brief introduction, he stopped by my desk more frequently to chat. I began to notice that some of the attorneys and assistants in the office were paying particular attention to my desk area. I knew there was probably some talk around the proverbial water cooler but it didn't bother me – we weren't doing anything we shouldn't be doing and if my life entertained them during their daily grind – so be it.

I enjoyed his company and he enjoyed mine. Sometimes we would meet for coffee in the lobby of the building with its grand marbled floor and suspended water structure flowing from the ceiling some thirty floors above us. It was during one of these coffee talks that we discovered that not only did we take the same commuter train home each day we also got off at the very same stop. As it turned out, his parents owned the house behind the one I rented for the boys and myself.

One day when he stopped by my desk to chat, I mentioned that I needed to go to an antique store on Charles Street during my lunch hour. I had seen a painting there the previous weekend and it was now haunting me in the way things can when they need to be purchased. (Yeah, I knew it was me haunting the painting and not the other way around but, in my defense, the painting started it.) He asked if he could join me and I said, "Sure, okay, fine with me."

Down on the street, he hailed a taxi for us. We climbed in and were on our way. In the cab we chattered and laughed as if we were off on a big adventure. Once the cab stopped, he paid the driver and we quickly climbed out. I could see the excitement in his eyes and in his gait - we were on a treasure hunt. He grabbed my hand and pulled me to the shop. At that moment I was struck by how handsome he was in his business suit and how, even at his age, he could make a bow tie look stylish. I thought it showed his playfulness and unique character.

He was really very sweet, and I could feel our flirting turning into something else. What exactly that was, still needed to be determined. But I was mindful of the fact that he was, and always would be fifteen years younger than I.

I was content with our friendship as it was – taking coffee together, enjoying a stroll along the Boston Harbor at lunchtime. It was nice to have someone to talk with about my life, my plans, and my parenthood. Christopher and Jonathan were in Elementary school and kept me busy with after school events and team sports. It wasn't easy being the only adult in the house, so my time at work and with him was cherished "me-time."

One day after work, instead of heading to the trains to go home, we headed out to the river in Newton. He said he wanted to show me a special place. When I asked him what made it special, he avoided the question and just whisked me along towards the river. I found myself with him on the bridge.

It was early October and the leaves were in peak foliage. The few that hung tight to their branches gave off just enough color to make it a spectacular view. We remained there for a while, just admiring the artistry of nature. As we continued along the bridge, I walked a few paces behind him. I could sense that he was in a contemplative mood –something was on his mind. He was dressed very solemnly from head to toe, with a black coat, black pants, and heavy black shoes. It impressed me how very European he looked. When we got to the end of the bridge we stopped and faced each other. After a long silent moment, he asked me if he could do something. Without much thought to what he meant I said, "Sure," and almost added, "I trust you." He then looked at me very tenderly, leaned over slowly and kissed me. It only lasted a few seconds but he was elated. I was a bit surprised and amused that he was so excited about it! He said he had wanted to do that for a very long time, that it had been consuming so much of his mind and that he was glad he had finally gotten it out of the way. It may have not been the most romantic denouement to our kiss but I understood what he meant.

Not long after, I found myself with him at the bridge again. But this time, I took him to the bridge.

We had both worked later than usual. The day gave way to a very cold autumn rain. I'd taken my car to work that day so I offered to give him a ride home – seeing as we lived so close to each other. As we drove through the streets of Boston you could see people on the sidewalks running with their coats pulled over their heads as to not get their work-dos wet. As we approached the river, on impulse, I pulled over and stopped. He looked at me with a 'hey, what gives' smile on his face. I insisted he come with me down the path to the bridge below. At first, he bemoaned the driving rain, that we had no umbrella, that the night was cold, and the evening late. But, I saw that his resistance was half-hearted and after a while, we got out of the car and made our way down to the river. By the time we got to the bridge we were soaking wet from the driving wind and rain. We, of course, were the only ones there. I felt as though we had the whole world to ourselves. It wasn't planned, or it was planned – I'm not so sure of which anymore - but we shared a long embrace and a kiss with so much passion that I almost forgot that it was cold, we were wet, and what my name was. I wanted him desperately and I knew he felt the same, but we both were beyond our boundaries and that made me uncomfortable. We must have stood there several minutes longer, wondering what was next but we knew it was time to go home.

Back at work, we continued our coffees in the lobby and walks around the city. Though are relationship had a more familiar dimension to it, we did not bring it to work with us.

Later that week, he invited me to go to his family's summer home in the woods on Cape Cod. He said his mother and aunt would be there and he'd love for them to meet me. I debated with myself as to whether I should go. I had the boys to consider and I wasn't sure how I would be received. The difference in our ages was always a splinter in my thoughts when I was with him. But he was wonderful and he was handsome and what was wrong with spending time with a person with those qualities? So, I made arrangements for a babysitter and told him, yes.

He picked me up in his jeep on Saturday morning and we headed southeast through the New England tree-lined expressway. I was happy to be away from the responsibility of parenthood and work for a time. I was happy that the day was so warm and beautiful that we could ride along with the top down and the wind in our hair. I was happy to be with him and that he was with me. I was happy.

Once over the Sagamore Bridge and onto the Cape we drove down a winding dirt road. We had been driving for an hour and it was getting close to noon. As we got closer to our destination, he told me that his grandfather had built the summer cottage and all his childhood memories revolved around growing up there. He told me about how he and his cousins helped build the walkway by bringing logs and stones up from the forest and how they would lie awake at night telling ghost stories to give themselves the heebie-jeebies.

At the end of the dirt road sat the cottage. The foundation was hand built with stones they had gathered as they cleared the land, and mortar. And, since it is rocky New England, the walkways and the hearth were also made of stone. The cottage, painted brick red, had a porch that ran the length of the front of the house and blocked the sun from gracing their door. Off to one side was an unattached little cottage, the size of a backyard shed for the children to play in - kind of like the biggest dollhouse I'd ever seen. We walked onto the darkened porch, and he led me though the door and into a wood paneled room. His mother and aunt sat at the kitchen table, preparing carrots and potatoes for the dinner. They looked up as we walked in. I saw their eyes meet mine, travel down my face to my chest, to my waist and legs, to my feet and back up again. I could see that they were not impressed. And I could not believe that they were related to this beautiful man. He introduced me and told them we had met at the law firm. Let's just say, it went downhill from there.

Without so much of a thought to who I was or where I had come from, they started to tell me how about the "people" they knew and who knew them and, basically, connecting popularity dots all over the room. Out of politeness I feigned interest and commented with the obligatory, "Oh?" and "Really?" "Uh-huh." But the obnoxious name dropping didn't bother me as much as the obvious implication that status, and people with status were more important than everyday existence and everyday people. Again, I was trying to understand how he came from them. And I could see by their pursed lips and narrowed eyes that they were trying to understand what he saw in me – they were not pleased with him and certainly not pleased with me.

When there was a pause in the one-sided conversation, he asked me to retrieve his bag from the backseat of the jeep. On my way down the walkway to the drive, I heard yelling from the cabin. It struck me that I had never heard him raise his voice before and was impressed with its strength. They spoke, or yelled Latvian so I could not understand what they were saying. But I wasn't naïve and knew it was about me – me and him to be exact. I retrieved his bag and hung outside by the jeep, listening to the argument get louder and louder.

When it stopped, he came barreling out the door, off the porch and to my side. Without speaking, he took me by the hand and led me down to the pond. We sat there for a few minutes in silence. I could see the anger and frustration in his face soften and turn to something else – sadness perhaps. "Shall we leave?" I asked. He just shook his head no.

Still holding my hand, he looked at me and told me that his mother and aunt found me to be very sweet - the fight hadn't been about me. It was about his breakup with his girlfriend, who happened to be younger than I was and in medical school, which I wasn't. So, in the end, the argument wasn't about who I was but who I wasn't. I suppose if I respected their opinion, I would have been upset. But I didn't and I wasn't. At that moment, the only person whose opinion matter was his. We sat for a few minutes longer. He released the argument from his thoughts with a shake of his head, straightening his back he said, "How 'bout a swim?"

I changed into my bathing suit in the children's cabin. As I slipped into the lace coral one-piece suit I had brought, I thought about the white two-piece bikini I almost brought. Since puberty I had always had a lot of curves, and the right proportions of breast and butt, which isn't a bad thing. It's only a bad thing when you feel you've already been judged and deemed unsuitable so, I was quite pleased and happy that my suit at the moment was a one piece, but still quite sexy.

The pond was down a narrow patch below the cabin about three hundred yards away. By the time I got to the pond's edge, he was already in the water up to his waist. I was hesitant to get in. I would only go up to my knees. As a young girl I would waterski in Salem Pond with Dad and Uncle Junior. But the last time I did, a large fish swam right between my legs, which gave me the creeps. So here, at his pond, I was a little leery about the fish underneath the surface, swimming around unseen and brushing against my thighs and swimming between my legs. I stood there for a long moment, ready to retreat to land. I tried to overcome my uneasiness by focusing on the beauty of the day, the leaves on the trees and the shimmering reflection on the still water from early afternoon sun. The smell of the air reminded me that we were far from the city, and all that came with it.

He stood yards from the water's edge, watching me. My fear gave way when I saw his big, beautiful eyes looking at me, his bare chest full and firm, and his arms outstretched, inviting me to him. I glided into the water and swam out to him. I felt liberated from the prior events – from everything before this moment. His mother and aunt no longer existed. The difference in our ages was nothing more than an unimportant detail. There was something very innocent and natural about us being together at this time, in this place. We swam around together, holding onto each other so as not to drift too far apart. Then he took me by the hand and gently pulled me towards him. As I glided along the water to him, he slipped his arms around my waist, held me up against his bare chest and kissed me. It was, in no uncertain terms, magical.

When it was time, he walked out of the water and across the grass to his towel. I watched from the water as he slowly dried himself off, the fluffy fabric caressing each muscle in his chest and then his arms and legs. When he was finished, he turned, picked up the other towel and held it out to me, beckoning me to come join him. And as I stepped from the pond, he gently placed the towel around my shoulders, snuggled me close, and kissed me on the cheek. God how I adored this man!

After we changed into dry clothes, he left me sitting on the porch as he went into house to tell his mother and aunt that we would not be joining them for supper. I could not hear their response but I imagine they were not happy. When he came out the door, I quickly stood and we walked back to the jeep. We stood by the door of the jeep, ready to get in, for a long time as he cradled me in his arms. I could tell he did not want to let me go – and, with all my heart, I did not want him to. At times he would loosen his hold and lean me back so he could see my eyes. I could see he was struggling with something he wanted to say. When the words wouldn't come, he would just gather me up again and we'd remain like that – engulfed in each other's presence.

When we got back to our life in the city, it began to happen a lot. We'd meet for coffee or dinner and in the middle of a conversation he would just sit and look at me intently. I could see he was in conflicted. At these moments I did not know how to help him. If he wasn't ready to tell me what was torturing him, I did not want to drag it out of him. That did not feel right. When the words did not come after a while his brow would furrow and he would move to another subject. In all truthfulness, I believe I knew what he was trying to tell me but he, obviously, wasn't ready, and I suppose, neither was I.

Weeks after I met his mother and aunt, he invited me to come and stay with him overnight at the cottage, though this time we would be alone. We had not taken our physical relation to the next level, and looking back and remembering our kisses and our embrace, I don't exactly know how or why. We were both holding back from taking the next step and I was worried that spending the entire night with him would be more than I could bear. I could not, however, resist his invitation and told him I would go.

We got to the cabin fairly late on a Friday night. It was a frosty night and all the leaves from weeks before were now long gone. He carried our overnight bags from the jeep to the house, unlocked the door, and turned on the lights. The paneled room where I had met his mother was now warm and inviting.

He brought our things up to his room, which still had the bunk beds from his youth. The beds were bare so I nervously helped him make up the tiny little top bunk with the sheets he brought from home. After the bed was made, we turned off the lights, climbed out of our clothes and onto the top bunk. When I asked him why he chose this room for us to sleep in, he said that as a young boy, he would lay in the top bunk, stare out the window at the night sky, look up at the stars and wonder who he would someday fall in love with.

"Tonight," he said, "I wanted to bring you to the stars and show them who it is."

It was a chilly fall night and the sheets were cold against our skin, but it didn't matter. He was nervous and so was I. I felt like a teenager again, sneaking a forbidden moment with my boyfriend. We kissed awhile and then we would just hold each other. The moonlight illuminated his skin and reminded me that this was the first time I had seen him naked. I was in awe and found the whole situation very surreal - as if it were happening to someone else or from a movie I'd seen. It was apparent that he wanted me, but I was afraid - afraid it would change our relationship. I was too old for him and I knew that. His family would forbid it and he knew that as well. The only thing I could see in our future, if we consummated our friendship in this way was heartbreak. If we had given into our desires that night it would have destroyed me, him, or us both. So, we just held each other and talked late into the night. He told me that for months he had been trying to tell me that he loved me. But he always stopped himself because it would never be acceptable to his family. He felt he owed a great debt to his father, who had worked hard to provide him with a Harvard education, and he could not disrespect his parents' wishes. He said he struggled with what was right and what was wrong. Because, philosophically, how could love be wrong?

We did not make love that night. And after he fell asleep, I crept downstairs and spent the rest of the night on the couch – though I didn't really sleep. One thought circled through my mind around and around and around, and that was, love was unfair. The next morning when he woke, he came downstairs and we gathered our things and left. The ride home was quiet until he broke the silence. "I want to give you something that no one can ever take away," he said.

It seemed as though we drove for an hour. When we stopped, we were in Falmouth, parked in front of a sweet, quaint old church. It was made of stone and stained glass and surrounded by beautifully-trimmed hedges. He came around my side of the Jeep and opened the door. He took me by the hand and walked me around the side of the building to the back lawn where we stopped and sat on a bench facing the ocean. "This is yours!" he said, waving an encompassing hand at the church. "You will always remember me when you are here and I will always be with you." Then he kissed me soft and sweet.

The next time I saw him, he took me to dinner in Harvard Square. He showed me where he used to row, and told me anecdotes about his college days. I listened to the sound of his voice and not so much his words. It was just enough to be with him again. On the Harvard Bridge we found ourselves dancing to a melody we created with our steps and our bodies. It was a full moon and the light danced off the Charles River. We twirled and dipped and slid across the bridge – a waltzing silhouette in the night. We danced as if no one was watching and as if there were no one else on earth. That was the last time I saw him.

When I remember how special he was, I realize that he really did give me that church. Or at least what it represented - love - sweet, unconditional love. It remains for me a beautiful memory of a beautiful man! And I can always be with him because within a moment there are many days.

Congressman Kennedy

I was hanging around the house, in-between temporary secretarial assignments and feeling as though my temporary work no longer suited my needs. I was itching to have a fulltime job, a job I could really call my own so, Jimmy introduced me to the event planner for Joe Kennedy, the Congressman from Massachusetts.

Starting out, I volunteered a couple of days a week answering phones, typing memos, and filing paperwork. It wasn't glamorous but it kept me busy and I hoped it would lead to something more. When a position did open up, I was asked if I like to interview for it, which I responded with a resounding, 'yes!' Though my enthusiasm was quickly extinguished when I learned I had to interview with the Finance Director.

I arrived twenty minutes early for my interview, dressed in a blue suit, and ready to show him that I was the right person for the job. When his secretary led me into his office, he merely sat behind his desk, waiting for me to approach. The office was rather nondescript – window, walls, desk, and the Director. He seemed to me to be your stereotypical, self-important, business hot-shot.

The first question he asked was, had I ever worked in a political office before? When I said, 'no,' he led me over to a wood-paneled wall with wall-to-wall framed photographs of him with prominent people such as politicians and celebrities. He called it – and I'm not making this up – his 'I Love Me' wall. I don't know if it was the name of the wall that repulsed me or the obvious worship of famous people in and around Boston. Or perhaps it was his blatant sexual harassment when he asked if I knew them, or if I did, had I had slept with any of them? I told him I had not had sex with any of them, to which he said, "I know one thing. You will have sex with me!"

At that point, I'd had enough. I stood up, picked up my coat and headed for the door. Following me, he made one last ditch effort to insult me by suggesting we get together sometime. To which I replied, "In your dreams. I don't want the job!" As I opened the door to escape, he pushed it shut, apologized, and told me to report to work on Monday. He would hire me at $25,000 a year. *So, had it all been some sort of a test?*

The Finance Director pretty much left me alone after that. Perhaps he understood, and I was very clear about it, that I was not the least bit interested in a dalliance with him. But, dogs being dogs, he wasn't always able to keep his inappropriateness to himself.

I had been working at 'Citizens for Joe Kennedy' in their Newton, Massachusetts office when I got on the elevator at the end of the day with the Finance Director and another man, who seemed to be as full of himself as the Director. I stood in the small elevator car with my face to the closed doors, clearly minding my own business. The other man, speaking to the Director, commented on how attractive the women in the office were. Out of the corner of my eye I could see the director looking at me. He then turned to the man and said, "Well, don't even try with this one - she's a lesbian!"

At first, I was shocked. Then I was ticked off!

As soon as I got home I called Jimmy and told him what had happened. I wanted more than anything to turn them both in for sexual harassment. I said I could file a complaint, file a lawsuit, and tell the world how they treated me and women in general. After he listened to my indignation and plans to bring justice pouring down on their heads, he advised me to let it go. He told me that they had enough money and plenty of lawyers to destroy me publically and financially. I knew he was right, but the saddest and hardest thing I had to come to terms with was that it did not matter how strong my case was – *they had the power*; that right and wrong were concepts people talked about, but those came at a cost I was unable to pay.

So, I let it go.

"Hello, I'm Joe"

My first week at the campaign office, I was sitting at my desk in the reception area answering phones when a tall, handsome man walked in. He came over to my desk, smiled, shook my hand and introduced himself. "Hello" he said, "I'm Joe!"

Now, I don't usually go gaga over celebs and famous people – though I've met a few - but seeing how he carried himself and the warmth of his smile and the confidence in his handshake, I now understood why people loved the Kennedy men.

After that initial meeting, Representative Kennedy would frequently come into the office to make phone calls to raise funds for his next campaign. Though asking people for money is never pleasant, I got a sense he didn't like doing it very much either. He would usually get pensive and snap back at Peter Maroney, who was usually stressed himself trying to find people to back the Congressman. Peter would brief him before the call; if they were previous donors, what they did for a living, who they knew, etc.

My job was full of interesting people and things to do. I was the assistant to the fund-raising director. She was tall, blond and beautiful both inside and out and I came to admire her quite a bit. The two of us had a riot together. To this day I regret not keeping journals of the hysterical antics that would play out in our office or at an event.

I loved the varied and unique experiences it afforded me. Each year I got to travel around the city, meeting new people – politicians, old-time Bostonians, and regular worker bees like me - as we planned and hosted fundraisers around Boston. One of the places we went to for events was Anthony's Pier 4. He was always having one event or another. When you enter the restaurant, you would notice an entire wall full of photographs of Anthony Athanas with movie stars and politicians. During the 1990s, it was truly a who's- who of Boston politics. It would not be unheard of to hear the proverbial, "I'll have so-n-so call you" or "I know so-n-so and I will hook you up.

Have your guy/girl, call my guy/girl..." and so on. If you could imagine an informal Wall Street boiler room with deals being made by the second, then that would pretty much describe how it was at Anthony's Pier 4 Restaurant.

One of my favorite duties was helping with Joe Kennedy's annual birthday party in Hyannis Port, the family home in Massachusetts. The parties usually had a theme and were always great fun to plan, as well as attend. One year the theme was the 'Wild West' and it was my assignment to go to the costume shop and pick up everyone's costumes. The one thing I remember most about the event was sitting and watching everyone dance the 'Macarena' in cowboy costumes. It certainly wasn't anything like the hoedowns in the cowboy movies I watched as a kid. I still laugh a little when I imagine those John Wayne wannabes in cowboy boots and spurs, hands on hips, moving to-and-fro to the beat and singing, "Heeey...Macarena!"

Unlike all the rumors that surrounded the Kennedy men, I never felt ill at ease in their presence, particularly Joe's. I was always treated with respect and acceptance, though I was not from the same social circle or background.

I once had to drive out to the Kennedy house in Hyannis Port to speak with Mrs. Kennedy about the color we were using to decorate a tent for a fundraising event. Someone on the decorating party saw the purple taffeta we were going to use for the ceiling and insisted that Mrs. Kennedy HATED the color purple. When I arrived at the house and knocked on the door, Congressman Kennedy answered the door. I explained my mission and he invited me in and told me to feel free to tour the house while I waited for his wife.

I couldn't believe I was actually walking around the Kennedy family home! I was surprised to find it was cozy, simple and warm. The fabrics were simple and floral. It was understated and not at all opulently decorated. There were pictures of the family yachting and playing football, and the family's favorite dog curled up on the floor. I would describe it as sweet. And I was quite humbled and in awe when I stood in one of the smaller bedrooms, looking at a photo of President Kennedy on the dresser, knowing that it was probably where he slept as a youngster.

After my tour of the house and getting what I had come for, Congressman Kennedy walked me to the door and we said our good-byes. After all the talk about Kennedy chauvinism and philandering, I was left with an impression of a very thoughtful, unassuming man who was very faithful to his wife, Beth.

The Finance Director once told me about an incident that happened when he and Joe were out of town on business. Joe had gone back to his hotel room at the end of dinner but the Finance Director lingered in the restaurant, finishing his meal. A beautiful girl who had been watching them throughout the evening came over to their table, handed him her hotel room key, and asked that he give it to Joe Kennedy. (Politicians, like rock stars have their groupies, particularly if you are a handsome Kennedy.) But the part of the story I found particularly impressive was that when the key was offered to Joe, he simply refused it and walked away. After hearing that story, Joe Kennedy became my hero – an example of the kind of man I wanted to meet and marry someday.

After working for the Kennedy campaign, meeting the man himself, and being privy to private moments I would, and still do, get upset when I hear the press bash him. I suppose it is part of being in public life, being a politician, and a Kennedy. The *Boston Globe* accused him of being stupid and a poor public speaker. Well, what do they know? Those are opinions, not facts. And regardless of their opinions, and their bashing, I still feel as though he would be a great leader for this country.

Congressman Kennedy left public office after his cousin Michael was killed in a skiing accident. I admire that his family life took precedence over public life. He did his time in Congress and gave a good amount of time to the public. Contrary to what the press said, I believe Joe Kennedy was smart – smart enough to get out of politics -- before it consumed him – just like George Washington. Unfortunately for me, when he left office, it meant that I was out of a job.

My last foray into the world of politics and corporate America was working for Massachusetts Development as the Executive Assistant to the Chief Executive Officer at the time. I had only been in my position for about six weeks when I took a call from a man who was very agitated. He barked at me impatiently, saying that my boss, "...needed to get in touch with Governor Romney – immediately!" Being a newbie, all I understood was that it had something to do with a project and the town of Harvard. He told me *they* were about to lose their lawsuit unless my boss, got through to the Governor. The

Governor had to change some legislation or a particular law so that the lawsuit would be ruled in their favor. Coming from the Kennedy campaign and seeing how it was run and in contrast to these shenanigans - I was shocked! The constant humming of the shredder, four and five times a day, sometimes, suddenly started to make sense. Shortly after that eye-opening experience, I decided that politics may be a job and a paycheck but it was time for a career change.

Growing up in America when I did had left me with the belief that we had a virtuous government and political system. Of co*urse, we do – why else would people from all over the world risk their lives to come here?* Boy, did I get a lesson.

What became clear to me was that the biggest tragedy for America was the legal system. Lawyers, politicians, public figures – all could be bought by corporations. If something doesn't suit their particular needs, they change the law to fulfill their greed.

How's that for the ultimate scam?

My boss, mentor, and friend John Cremens

Jonathan's dad, Jimmy, a great dad to both my boys

Congressman Joe Kennedy shaking my hand during his campaign

Congressman Kennedy and his wife Beth do the 'Macarena

Me (C) and friends at a Kennedy fund-raiser

Jonathan and Christopher in Boston

Chapter 7: The Mask of Death

For God so loved the world, that he gave his only begotten Son, that whosoever believeth in him should not perish, but have everlasting life.
– John 3:16

My Father's Conversion

Dad and I were never really very close. I felt mostly ignored as a child and he was not a man to share his feelings or show affection. I found out in 1996 that he was dying of cancer and in a lot of pain, though he refused the morphine that was offered to him. He was also experiencing horrible visions and dreams. When I spoke with him on the phone, I could sense his fear and asked him, plainly, if he was afraid to die. He said he was. There was clearly not a lot I could do for him that would alleviate his pain and fear, except share with him the peace I found in my faith.

My father had been baptized a Mormon but never practiced the faith or raised his children to believe in it – and I was okay with that. From my perspective, faith isn't something you inherit, like the shape of your parent's nose, the color of their eyes, or the purse of their lips. Faith is something you believe to be true deep in your soul. And no amount of pulling, shaking, or prying can loosen its hold. And that's what I wanted for my father. I knew if I could bring him to my faith, it would ease some of his anxiety and provide comfort; the comfort in knowing a merciful God, and looking forward to a homecoming.

I felt uncomfortable whenever I had to talk to him about anything important - our relationship was really not that kind - especially the subject of faith and religion. So, I wrote him a letter asking if he would consider letting Father Isaac, the monk, who had cured Christopher, read prayers over him. At the time, I wasn't even sure I mailed it and was pretty sure I hadn't, until I called to check on his health and Mom told me he wanted to talk to me. Speaking to him on the phone that night, I asked him to convert to the Greek Orthodox faith. I sensed a hesitation, that unspoken, cowboy, resistance to the idea. I wasn't sure what was keeping him from agreeing to it but I thought, *if he won't do it for himself, perhaps he would do it for me.* I asked him to consider it a gift, a reconciliation of sorts, to me. I told him that it would mean a lot to me. When he finally agreed, I could see that a big weight had been lifted from his shoulders. I could postulate what it meant, but, in the end, it is merely a projection of what I hoped was in his heart – conversion to faith through prayer – which had become an imperative to my life. I immediately set about making the arrangements.

It was more than fortunate that a monk from the Church was planning a trip west at the very same time my father needed help. I contacted him at the monastery and he agreed to stop in Utah. Once again, my faith in divine intervention was strengthened. I saw all the seemingly disparate events come together, in a single moment of time, to bring a dying man closer to God. I could chalk it up to coincidence, but in my heart, I knew that it was much more than that.

When Father Panteleimon, the monk, arrived in Salt Lake City, I was still in Boston, anxiously waiting by the telephone and praying that he wouldn't back out at the last minute. Dad was too sick and weak to leave the house, so the service was performed in my parents' living room. The man who had told me about the monastery and the monk was there, as was his wife and daughter, and my mother.

Father Panteleimon prepared my father for his baptism by reading prayers over him and anointing him with holy oil from the Holy Sepulcher[ix] in Jerusalem. During a typical baptism in the Eastern Orthodox Church, the baby or person is immersed in water to symbolize being cleansed in the River Jordan where Jesus was baptized. Since my father was so very sick, feeble, and wracked with pain, he was anointed with oil instead.

I was anxious to hear and finally received a call from my mother. She said the baptism was beautiful. When my father got on the phone, I noticed that his voice had changed. It was not weak and fearful. He told me that he felt wonderful and at peace; that his pain was gone both emotionally and physically. He thanked me and told me how much he loved me.

I was amazed and astounded when the photographs of the baptismal ceremony came back from the developer. In one of the photos, as Father Panteleimon anointed my father with the holy oil, a white light shined down from somewhere above the priest and fell directly on my father. My mother said that Dad sat in his chair, head bowed and bathed in light, and she could his face, which, because of the cancer, had become strained with pain and fear, relaxed and shined with an incredible peace and love. From the moment of his anointing, she said, the pain he felt throughout his body just stopped – *it just disappeared*. Dad told Mom that had he known what had been revealed to him that day, he would have prayed much harder for those he loved his whole life. He no longer was afraid to die and, in fact, could not wait to see death. I know in my heart that Dad's baptism was one of the many miracles I'd experienced.

Not long after that, I returned home to Utah, and I would sit with Dad and read prayers. Never in my life did I expect to be sharing this kind of closeness with my father, particularly with so much spirituality.

The truth be told, I had feared him my entire life. He loomed large over me as a child, and as an adult. To me he was very tall and strong at six-foot-four inches and two hundred and forty pounds. He was a decorated soldier during the Korean War but he never spoke about his days in battle. And beyond his physical presence, he was very hard on his children. We felt as though we never quite met his expectations. There was a distance that he put between us and him. He would, at times, widen the divide by being callous. He had once told me, when I was preparing to register for a college course that there was no point because I was stupid and unable to learn anyway. I often wonder if it was me he meant to say shouldn't go to college or women in general. Perhaps he was a bit envious of my mother's success and was trying to make sure that didn't happen to my husband. Unfortunately, I was never able to have those questions answered, even after our bonding in the Church.

Years later, after his death, I learned that he had a child from his first marriage who died in his very arms. I cannot imagine the pain that must have caused him and he never spoke of it. But with that little piece of history, of knowledge, I think I now understand why he was unable to be close to us, his children.

The Miracle Christmas

The boys and I arrived in Salt Lake City between Thanksgiving and Christmas. It would be the last holiday I would share with my father.

When we arrived, the whole family, including my brother and sister, had gathered to be by Dad's side and give him support. As a young girl, I thought he was the strongest man in the world, so it was difficult to see him so emaciated and weak.

A day or two after we arrived, Christopher, who was fifteen years old by then, began complaining of stomach pain and nausea. He had a fever and the chills so I put him up in my old bedroom at my parent's house to rest. There had been a flu outbreak in Boston a few weeks before our trip so I assumed he had caught a nasty bug. Over the course of the next two weeks, I went from my father's bedroom to Chris' bedroom tending to one and then the other. I would get up in the morning and go sit with my father for a few hours, then I would check on Christopher, taking his temperature, giving him aspirin, and trying to get him to eat. Some days he felt better than others but he still lacked an appetite.

On Christmas Eve, my stepsister came to the house to visit my father. When she heard that Christopher was ill, she went up to check on him. Unbeknownst to me, he had started to spit up blood. When she came downstairs to tell me, I could barely comprehend what she was saying. I had just been in his room a short while before and there was no indication that he was really that sick. I'm sure she could see my shock and helped me with getting him to the hospital, fortunately, only five minutes away.

The hospital was quiet, as one would expect at 10:00 PM on Christmas Eve. They wheeled Christopher into an exam room and took his temperature and blood pressure, listened to his heart and his belly. I was sat with him as they did the initial triage. The nurse said he that his blood pressure was high as was his temperature. Shortly after, they quickly wheeled him down the hall to another room to do an ultrasound. I followed along and waited inside the room. When they allowed me in, I sat in the quiet, dark x-ray lab holding my son's hand. He lay on the hard, cold table, very pale and very ill. He was very weak and said nothing. From somewhere nearby, I heard a woman, whether it was a nurse, a technician, or radiologist, I don't know, call for a surgeon.

"STAT!"

The word made my heart stop and my stomach sink.

Within a half an hour a tall, balding man in a casual jacket with 'Members Only' sewn above the pocket and wearing a blue baseball cap walked into the room. He looked at the glowing pictures of my son's insides, turned to the nurse and told her to prepare for surgery. He then turned to me.

"Are you his mother?" he asked.

"Yes," was the only word I could manage to speak.

"Well, prepare for a long night," he said and left.

They rolled Christopher to the elevator to take him to the surgical floor. The nurse escorted me to the waiting room where I proceeded to stretch out on the couch. I was exhausted and the only one in the whole hospital holding vigil for a loved one in surgery on Christmas Eve. I couldn't grasp what was happening. How could Christopher be so sick that he needed surgery? He had been ill with the flu -so I thought - but he never let on that he was in pain. He never told me that he had been spitting up blood. I searched my mind for what I had missed, for some hint, some indication that it was not the flu and he had been getting worse and so very ill. I came up with nothing.

My heart ached at the thought of Christopher laying just two doors down from where my father lay dying, never saying a word -- just suffering in silence! Now, after years of reflection on this episode, I have come to believe, in my heart, that my son had not complained about his pain so as not to distract me or the family from my father's and his grandfather's last days. As I stared at the ceiling, one question circled through my mind without response or reprieve. I was losing my father to cancer at any moment. Would I lose my son, too?

I did not know that I had fallen asleep on the couch until I felt someone tap the side of my red cowboy boot. It must have been around 4:00 AM when I saw the Doctor in surgical garb smiling down on me. Before I could pull myself up from the sleeping depths, he turned and walked out of the room.

An hour later a nurse from the recovery room came in and told me my son was out of surgery and in the Intensive Care Unit. His appendix had burst, releasing its poison into his little body and causing peritonitis. Dr. Belnap removed as many organs as possible, flushed them out, and replaced them. However, there were lots of places inside the body where the infection could hide and Christopher would probably need many more surgeries. Dr. Belknap had also called in a team of infection experts. The bottom line was, he was going to be a very sick boy.

Before she left, she wanted me to know how very lucky I was to have Dr. Belnap as my surgeon. She told me he was an excellent pancreatic transplant surgeon, who had just happened to volunteer for Christmas Eve duty so the married surgeons could be home with their families. Again, I saw my beliefs demonstrated in my life. Others may have seen a coincidence in it being Christmas Eve and having the best doctor possible for my son's condition available, but I didn't. I knew whose hand was holding mine and it gave me strength to deal with the challenges I knew were coming my way.

By the time I was allowed to visit Christopher in the ICU, it was Christmas morning. He lay there with tubes coming from his nose, his incision and his penis. Though he was asleep and on medication, I could see the pain in his face. I stood by his bed, stroking his hair and holding his hand until I felt calm enough to leave him.

I had been so distraught at the hospital, I forgot that it was Christmas and Santa had to put presents under the tree. I felt awful, physically and emotionally, as I raced home to Jonathan who, at five years old, was now a big fan of Santa. When I got home, he was standing at the front door crying for me as I walked in. His little world had been turned upside down and he wanted an explanation. Through his tears and sniffles, he asked for his brother. I told him that Christopher was in the hospital getting better. Jonathan asked why Santa hadn't come. I told him that he did not want to wake up Grandpa and was waiting for me to help. I grabbed the presents I had bought, wrapped, and hidden. I put them under the tree in the living room. I watched Jonathan's excitement as he ripped off the Christmas wrap and squirm with impatience for another and another, the image of Christopher in the ICU bed superimposed itself on the morning events.

After the presents were opened, it was me who was squirming with impatience. I needed to get back to the hospital. Jon asked if we could take Christopher's presents to him in the hospital, to which I said, "Absolutely!" I ran upstairs to shower and change, checked on my father, dressed Jonathan in the new duds he got from Santa, buckled him the car seat, and left. And that would be my daily routine for the unforeseeable future.

For the next week, I ran from home to the hospital and back again trying to be in two places at once. My father remained on the edge of death and I feared Christopher did, too. He lost so much weight that his face was sharp and hallow, and his body rawboned. He lay in the hospital bed – now too big for him - listless, ashen and weak. He seemed so frail and vulnerable that it made my heart weep. As I sat by his bed, straightening his bedclothes and his hair, I was frustrated that I could not do more. There was a time when a kiss on the forehead or on a boo-boo could make everything, all better. But that mother's magic did not work here. Here it was the doctors, the nurses, the drugs, and the scalpels that I prayed would make my son better. I could not help but draw a parallel between the monk, who cured Christopher of his seizures, and the doctor who saved his life on Christmas Eve. They would be forever in my heart and in my debt.

Eight days after Christopher's emergency surgery, the peritonitis would not let go its hold on him. Another surgery was scheduled. Again, I found myself in the waiting room on the surgical floor, nervously sitting, standing, pacing, and walking the halls. I found myself asking God how much, how long, how many must my trials be? I reflected on it being New Year's Eve; a day of hope for a new year and new beginnings. Perhaps it was an omen – Christopher having another operation on the eve of another meaningful event. I knew I was grasping for something, anything that would tilt the outcome in his favor.

Christopher made it through his second surgery but remained in the hospital. It had been two weeks of traveling between home and the hospital. At times I would not make it home to eat or visit my father. My mother, sister, aunt and others would bring food, and Jonathan to the hospital just so I could eat so and he could visit his brother. I saw the toll it all was taking on my mother. Her beloved husband and now her sweet grandson! It was almost all too much for us.

On January 7th while my son was still in the hospital, my father, with his family by his side, succumbed to cancer. Or was it death? I was relieved that his suffering was over and happy that he had gone home but I missed him terribly, and still do.

Dr. Belnap released Chris from the hospital in time to attend my father's funeral. But before we left, he stressed that Christopher would, more than likely, need more surgeries. He explained that there was no way of knowing how much bacteria were still hiding in his body.

And, as if that wasn't frightening enough, I had no idea how the surgeries, the hospitalization, and the follow-up care were going to get paid. I had no insurance. I was a struggling, single mother. *I used God as my insurance carrier.* I would have to be like Scarlet O'Hara – "I can't think about that right now. If I do, I'll go crazy. I'll think about that tomorrow."

Shortly after we buried my father, Chris broke out with yet another fever. I sat by his bed all night praying to the Virgin Mother. I remembered reading somewhere that if you ask the Holy Mother to direct your prayers to Jesus, she always hear you and honor your request. Watching her son Jesus die was so painful, so heart-wrenching, so excruciating, she promised his death would not be in vain. She is a great intercessor for those who ask for her help. In fact, it is believed that it is an insult to her if you do not believe she will help. I prayed all night to heal my son. The next day, his fever broke. The Holy Mother kept her promise.

The boys and I had been in Utah for over a month and it was time to get back home Boston to work and to school. After Dr. Belnap reexamined Chris, he christened him well enough to travel back to Boston.

A few months later, I called the hospital to check on the bill, which was something I dreaded but could not put off forever. Someone in the finance department told me that the cost was over fifteen thousand dollars - and that was just due the hospital! As dismayed as I was, I vowed that I would scrimp together the money – though it would be difficult and might take me the rest of my life – but I would repay these people for saving my son. When I asked about the surgeon's fees, I was told that it was a mere two thousand dollars. Dr. Belnap had only charged a thousand dollars for each of the surgeries on Christmas and New Years' Eve. I was awash with such gratitude for the man who expertly cared for Christopher and then charged a small fraction of his fees. What can you say to a man who saves your son and your livelihood afterwards? For that, he will always and forever be in my prayers.

A few days later proved, for me, to be the other miracle in this event. I called the hospital to arrange a payment plan for the hospital bill – all fifteen thousand dollars of it.

I waited a while on the line listening to the telephone Muzak. I waited and waited, and waited, ready to accept the bad news. A woman finally got on the phone and said the hospital had taken care of the bill. I did not owe them anything – no money! I could not get the phrase out of my head. It was like a tune that gets stuck in your head and plays over and over again. I DID NOT OWE THE MONEY! I DID NOT OWE THE MONEY! I DID NOT OWE THE MONEY! I was reminded once again that God so loves us, if we just believe, He will help. If it doesn't happen right away, that's okay. It's because He has something greater in store for us. We will receive what He intends at a later time. Just have faith.

We returned to Boston. Chris went back to school. And there were no more nightmares. We settled back into our family routine and our financial reality. I worked my butt off to do a good job and be home on time from work. I did homework with the kids in the evenings, went to soccer and football practices during the week, and games on the weekends. I monitored their television and talked with them about making the right choices in friends. Occasionally I would come up short with cash for the necessities and have to count out the change for milk and lunch money, while trying not to forget the homeless and beggars on the street. It was important to me that I help the less fortunate whenever I could. Sometimes I would pray to make the rent and hoped the $500 car I bought wouldn't break down. But, regardless of the struggle, I took solace in the fact that my sons were healthy, in an incredible school system and had the world at their feet. What more could a mother want?

However, it was short lived. Not long after that Mom started getting sick and during a vacation she shared with the family that she too, had been diagnosed with leiomyosarcoma – a fatal cancer and wasn't expected to live long. She would soon be joining my father. *Here we go again.*

Thank God for the family farmhouse next door to her. I had to get back to Utah now to be with my mother. Christopher was in high school, Jonathan in the last year of elementary school so, I packed up our things once more, and away we went again. To Utah.

Dad's Premonition

One evening while Christopher lay in the hospital fighting the infection that was trying to take over his body and my father lay at home, close to death, I sat next to his bed praying with him. We were in the middle of prayer when Dad began to scream in terror. His eyes were wide and full of fear. I was reminded of my Aunt Clee and the look of horror left on her face even after she was gone. Panicking, I asked, "What's the matter, Dad?! What is it?!"

Without seeming to be aware of my presence he wailed, "The people! Oh my God, all those poor people!"

Believing he had become delusional from the heavy doses of pain medication, I tried to calm him by reassuring him that I was there. But he ranted on in such pain and anguish that my eyes filled with tears.

"The planes are hitting the towers! People are jumping out the buildings! Oh my God! All those people are burning!"

It was a brutally detailed and horrifying vision. I was instantly reminded of my own vision of hell when I was a young girl. It pained me to think of it, but what my father was imagining was just too similar.

My father had told me during one of our prayer readings that he would die on Christmas, though, Christmas had come and gone and he was still hanging on to life. In the Orthodox Christian religion, which my father had converted to, on the Julian calendar[x], Christmas is celebrated on January 7th. And, so it was, after the awful vision had been forgotten, and with his loving family by his side, my father passed away on January 7th at 3:00 AM the very same time as the Russian Bishop Goury[xi] - Orthodox Christmas day.

Five years after my father died, I was in Boston staying with a friend who lived on Union Wharf. The bedroom I was in faced Logan Airport and I was lying in bed when Jonathan, who was staying with his Dad at the time, called to tell me he was on his way to school. I looked at the clock and it was 8:00 in the morning. I watched as the planes took off from Logan while we chatted. After we said good-bye I got up and walked to the North End to get a morning cup of coffee.

There was an unusual amount of people gathered at a television set in one of the restaurants. A man told me that two planes had hit one of the Towers at the World Trade Center in New York. I watched in horror when a few minutes later, the Pentagon was attacked. As the morning events unfolded, the reports became more and more ominous and frightening. I became glued to the television. I watched the news, along with the rest of the world, and saw the jet planes hitting the World Trade Center towers over and over and over again in a perpetual newsreel rewind. It was then I realized that I was experiencing the true horror of my father's vision. On September 11th, 2001, I mourned for thousands of people who lost their lives, the citizens of the United States who lost their sense of security, the world for the repercussions that would follow, and for my father who wasn't alive to witness the most heinous event in recent human history – the very vision he saw on the sunset of his life.

The moment of his anointing with Holy oil, an unexplained shaft of light fell on my father

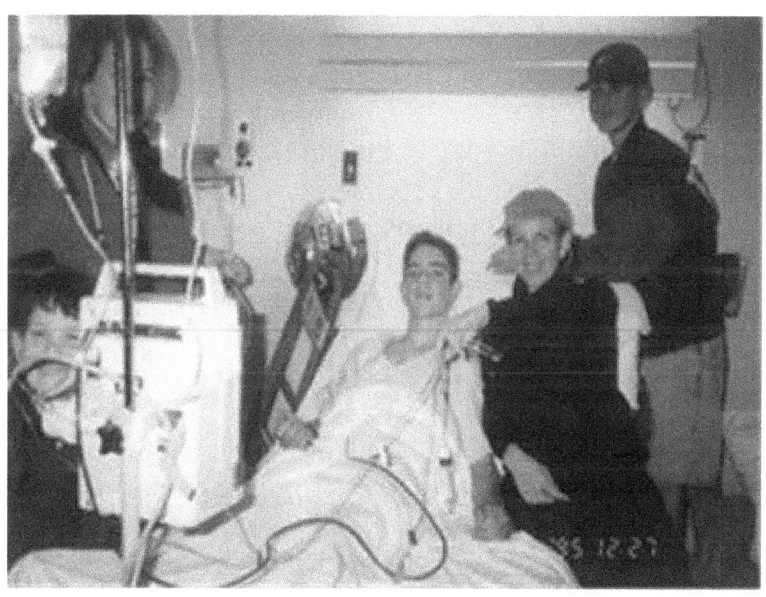

The Christmas miracle – Jonathan (L), Chris (C), me, and cousins

Chapter 8: Heaven, Hell, & Hollywood

Again, the devil took him to a very high mountain and showed him all the kingdoms of the world and their splendor.
"All this I will give you," he said, "if you will bow down and worship me." Jesus said to him, "Away from me, Satan! For it is written: 'Worship the Lord your God, and serve him only.' Then the devil left him, and angels came and attended him. – Matthew 4:8-11

My Happy Place

Several years before my father died when I was living in Boston after Jonathan was born, I received a call from my father. He told me that he and my mother were talking and they had a proposition. He asked if I would consider moving back to Salt Lake City, if they would sell me the land next door – the farmhouse I rented off and on over the years and loved. The price was tempting - $64,000 – but I really didn't have that kind of money at the time, so I told him I would think about it.

When I told Jimmy about my mother's illness and my father's proposal from years ago, he called my mother and offered to help the boys and me move in, and build an extension onto the house. When my mother took him up on his offer, I moved back to Salt Lake and began making house payments on the land I had loved so much over the years; the old barn with the fireplace of bottles and inlaid dinosaur bones was one of my favorite aspects of the property. With Jimmy's support, I built a breezeway from the old farmhouse to the barn, which came to be the living room.

After everything was renovated and redesigned, the farm became my *happy place*. The smell in the air from fresh pine trees was remarkable. Creek water elms that stood 50-feet high surrounded the property and, in the spring, had a wonderful fragrance that seemed to wake all the other trees. And when the winter gave way to the earth anew, I would wake early in the morning around dawn, check on the boys to make sure they were covered and warm - and still breathing (a quirky mother thing to do), slip into the rubber boots I got from my father - duck hunting waders that went up to my butt – and then while still in my robe, I'd, head out to feed my critters, with my International Coffee (*for those special moments*) in hand.

Within a year, we adopted a potbelly pig, two white ducks, a horse, and a lamb. Grunt, our pig, always needed to be called for breakfast. Chris had made him a small house, similar to a dog house, with a straw floor and bed. He would lie inside until he heard me call to him in my deepest voice, "Come – come - come – come – come!" I would often repeat until he saw the ducks, Dally and Dolly, waddling toward me. Then he would, hesitantly, shake the sawdust from his back, let out a grunt or two – hence his name - and then saunter towards the pig pellets.

On my farm, the ducks got seed, Grunt got pellets, and the horse got hay and a bucket of oats, which I would take a pinch of for myself sometimes. They tasted better than oatmeal. Oftentimes, I'd have to climb under the railing and walk through the mushy ground of dirt, hay, urine, and water - but I loved it. One of my favorite farm chores was grooming my horse. I loved the feel of the brush on her long, black, muscular neck, and looking into her big brown eyes, kissing her warm nose good morning, and lightly teasing her nose whiskers with the end of my finger. If it was warm enough, I'd spend my quiet time in the hammock with my coffee, waiting for Izzy my lamb to finish her grazing. After which she would join me on the lawn and laying beneath the hammock while I tickled her between her eyes. For me, life did not get any better than that.

Between my first and second cup of coffee, I'd walk the property and smell the apple blossoms or whatever was in bloom at the time. We had lilacs and cherry blossoms, a large willow tree that held the hammock, a Blue Jasper tree that stood 100 feet tall, holly bushes, and two pine trees I planted - one for each of my sons when they were born. My Uncle Lamar, who at the time was the head of Grand Canyon National Park, gave me the pines to plant in memory of the boys. He said it was so they would grow tall, straight, and strong, and be as grand as the Canyon herself.

To enhance the landscape and because I love design, I put in 1000 square feet of sod with the help of my mother and my aunt Aggie. I planted all kinds of flowers and ivy that grew up the trunk of the apple tree, which, Bodie, my tree-climbing dog used to play in. To keep all the critters off the new plantings, Christopher and I built a fence. Then we dug a big pond, found an old rusted coal stove, and made it into a waterfall that drained back into the pond. It was really quite beautiful.

We had created such a wondrous Garden of Eden that one summer day we were surprised to find two mallard ducks had made it their home. And since we already had Dally and Dolly, the white ducks, it was only fitting that we name the mallards Mally and Cally. And that's how we ended up with Dally, Dolly, Mally, and Cally. But it was all good, because there is nothing closer to God on earth than being with the world He created and caring for His creatures.

Another creature God gave me to care for was Blackie, my horse. Sometimes I'd let her out of her stall and just watch as she ran a fast as she could around the property, kicking, rearing, and horse playing (and that's why your mom says no horseplay in the house). For a special treat, I would let her graze on the lawn, which was typically off limits, before putting her back into the pasture. But then I found out that even horses can be spoiled if you aren't careful. This particular day I forgot to close the French doors, perhaps just airing out the house. I was in the kitchen cooking or cleaning when I heard a large clinking noise on the tile behind me. When I turned around, there was Blackie. She had come through the open doors, into the house, and was making her way to the kitchen. I jokingly scolded her as I lead her back to her stall. I thought that she might have been jealous that I sometimes let Izzy into the house to watch TV with me.

The farm also gave me a safe and wonderful place to raise my boys. They had almost two acres of land to play around on, numerous trees to climb, and a barn to play in. In the winter they would use Mom's and Dad's snowmobiles to ride around the yard. It was nice to have them so close and within view as they played and grew.

With a wide circle of friends, most people would drop by to visit and watch me, the boys, and the critters. They would often comment on how lucky I was. And I was. Sometimes, friends would show up who were having some sort of life problem. When they shared their troubles with me, I listened and provided what little comfort I could. It was gratifying to me that after sitting with me for a while they always left in a better state of mind.

I lived at the farmhouse for years, raising my two boys next door to my mother, and visiting with friends. I felt as though I had finally made myself a happy place, which I called 'La-la Land.' When my Mom was sick and I would go over to her house to help her, but it seemed she was really holding her own. I was content.

So, with the boys in school all day and plenty of time on my hands, I decided to get a part time job in Park City.

Blair and the Red Flags

Although I was preparing for the eventual death of my mother, I had come to know a great inner peace. I enjoyed my job in Park City, I was meeting fun people. The boys were doing well and I was preparing the path to becoming a nun. Then one day, a dark-haired man came into the store. I greeted him as I did all my customers. We chatted a little, though I remember about what, and he left. Looking back, I wish I had remembered my Aunt Clee's warning before her death. She told me to beware of a dark-haired man I would meet at work. I guess, obviously, I did not take her clairvoyant words seriously.

The next day when I came into work, my manager told me that a man had called looking for me – twice – and had left his number. I told her I wasn't interested in calling him back; I had no idea who he was. When he called again, I happened to answer. He introduced himself as Blair, the man from the day before. He asked if I wanted to go skiing with him on my next day off. I wasn't really interested so I told him I'd think about it, though my manager said I should go. He was persistent and insistent, and after many phone calls pleas, I agreed to meet him for a drink in Deer Valley, an upscale ski resort area near Salt Lake City.

By the time I walked into the bar, he was sitting next to a stone fireplace with a drink in his hand. He looked like shit. I remember thinking that he was better looking in the store. He sported large, dark patches under his eyes that twinkled with the glossiness of too many glasses of scotch. When he saw me, he gave me a wave and a wry (or rye) grin. I took a seat in the chair across from him; he motioned for the waitress to come over. I ordered a glass of wine and settled in for an uneventful night next to the warm fire.

We talked about typical first-date kind of stuff – the view of a person's life from a thousand feet up. He actually did most of the talking, and mostly about himself. After listening to him talk about himself, his company and growing up in Montauk New York, he told me that his father was the head physician at some big hospital in New York. He had been married and had two daughters.

I told him about my vow to become a nun, that I was never going to marry again, and that when Jonathan was out of the house, I was going to enter a convent. I told him about my discussion with my father confessor and my desire to be a nun, and about the day I went into the chapel at my church and told God I would someday leave the world and devote myself to living a life of poverty, chastity and obedience. I was pleased when he did not refute me and began asking questions about my faith and my church. He asked who had the authority to change my vows or my decision. I told him about the monk who saved my son and the monastery in Massachusetts. Little did I realize that he would be on the phone to my priest the very next day, asking if he could date me. I was surprised he even got ahold of him. He is a very busy man and travels around the world to feed his spiritual flock. To my utter surprise, he was given consent.

Two glasses of wine later, it was time for me to leave. He insisted on walking me to my car, which was gentlemanly. It must have been the two glasses of wine, because though he turned me off, as I opened my car door he grabbed and kissed me. I was a bit offended by his brazenness, but it was an okay kiss. Maybe it was chemistry or maybe it was loneliness. Or maybe it was just plain lunacy. A few days later I got a call from my priest in Boston. He called to find out my thoughts on my dating Blair. I reminded him that I had made a vow. He told me that perhaps it wasn't God's will and I should at least see how it went. I was saddened and frustrated when he told me that I was too young, too attractive to make that kind of commitment. He advised me to wait and reminded me that I had two boys who, though older, needed a father in their lives. He encouraged me to begin dating again.

Our next date went very well. Something had changed with me and perhaps with him. We were really beginning to connect, and after a couple of weeks, we became inseparable. Not a day went by that we did not talk on the phone and make arrangements to be together.

Then one day, I got a huge RED FLAG -- you know, one of those 'uh-oh' feelings when someone says or does something, and you say to yourself – 'well, there's something wrong here.' But your heart wants what your hearts wants and it makes those red flags, those warning signs, seem like nothing more than pesky little *not-going-to-rain-on-my-parade* gnats. And you push them down and shoe them away; just so you can follow your heart, where ever it may lead. And, if your head doesn't want to follow, well then to hell with it, who needs it anyway. Well, this was one of those times.

I was at work at the store. A tall blonde woman came in and told me that her friend had just been dumped by Blair for me. And, if that wasn't devastating enough, her mother had just passed away. I was in shock. He had never talked about this girl. *'How much could she have meant to him if he never told me about her?' I thought.* (Red flag successfully avoided!)

I asked him about her when he came home. He told me that she had a bad crush on him and he was never really interested in her, he felt bad for her because of her losing her mom so just tried to stay out of the picture and be kind. She must have taken it the wrong way.

With the issue of the other woman - which was me without realizing it – dealt with, Blair and I continued dating. We skied together. We dined together. He came to my house and I went to his. He'd serenade me on his guitar. He was great with my sons, and everyone who saw us together, remarked how in love we were. I was so high on my relationship with Blair that I couldn't imagine ever being without him. If you had asked me before him if it were possible to love someone that much, I would have emphatically said, no! To no one's surprise, within two months, we were engaged.

In a traditional and Hallmark moment, on Valentine's Day morning, he got down on one knee and asked me to marry him. Well, for the first time in years I trusted men again and let myself fall in love. Certainly, this had to be a good guy, hopefully not a cheat and a liar like all the others I had dated over the years. I just kept on believing that a decent guy must be out there. He even agreed to become baptized in my church so I could continue to receive communion. The more I was with him the more I felt that he was most likely sent to me from God!

After I had accepted his marriage proposal, then things starting to get weird. He was spending more and more time at the condo in Park City without coming down to Salt Lake City after work.

Then one day a childhood friend of his came for a visit. I drove up to Park City and found them sitting in Blair's car. I pulled up alongside. *They*, and, yes, I mean they, told me that *they* felt it best if we called off the marriage. His friend from Newport, Rhode Island said that I was not Blair's type. I couldn't believe it – *they* were calling it off from his car window? Now, that's real class.

I went home and bawled my eyes out. I didn't dare tell my mom. She was very sick from cancer and the treatments, and her greatest wish was to see me married to a nice guy before she died. She really loved Blair and so did I. I don't know how but I talked him into it getting back together. I accepted the blame for the whole thing falling apart. I told him that I was off because of the stress of taking care of my mother, that I knew I wasn't the fun girl he had known but to please give me another chance. I promised that things would be better if he would just give me another chance.

Our relationship resumed. We were dating in January at the Sundance Film Festival, engaged by February, and set our wedding day for several months later, June 6, 1999, or "D" day, as my son Jonathan called it. It was his clever way of telling me that I was headed for disaster.

We decided to get married at the farm. We decorated the farmyard, the horse, the ducks, the lamb and the pigs; everything and every critter was dressed for the occasion and wearing a collar made of flowers. Blair's daughters, their friends and my nieces were the flower girls. The small chapel in the back yard was decorated and tents set up for the occasion. It was a beautiful scene and a beautiful day, until a dark, gloomy cloud moved in from the west.

I was getting dressed in the bedroom, my dear friends, BJ and Betty, were there to help with my hair, my makeup and my dress. When BJ left the room, I confided in Betty, I didn't feel right about this marriage. I told her that I had the strongest inclination to run. She knew me well and could tell I was tuned into something, something wrong with this relationship. She said she could get the car and pull it up front. I could sneak out the front door while everyone expected me to come out the back, then we could take off. She said it would take a while for them to notice I wasn't going through with it. But I thought about my mom, my boys, and all the drama that would follow. In the end I could not just leave them all hanging, so I went out the back door, never bothering to fix my hair.

The setting was magically beautiful, if the view of my impending marriage wasn't. There were flowers everywhere, including on the farm critters who were dressed in crowns of flowers. Especially meaningful and inspiring to me were the Greek Orthodox priests who came from Washington and Boston to do the service.

Mom was very sick at the time but was able to attend. The priest who performed the ceremony informed the guests of my mother's condition and said that the marriage was due to her fervent prayers, she had so badly wanted to see me happily married. She seemed so happy. So, I chose to believe and trust that I had a man who loved me and my boys. And he was very exceedingly kind to my mother, who he knew, was suffering.

Blair would often attend church with me and would even try to chant, which is part of the Greek Orthodox ritual. He became, to me, the most charming and romantic man I had ever met. To this day, I am sometimes haunted by the memory of him looking at me and mouthing the words 'I LOVE YOU' whenever he'd catch my eye.

Mom lived two doors down from my little farm. As her cancer progressed, she became more and more ill and unable to care for herself. I began staying at her house during the day while the boys were in school. Most days, after tending to my mother, I'd gather up the boys after school and drive to Park City, which was about forty minutes away. Blair had a condo there and worked as a Risk Management specialist in the stock and bond markets. Oftentimes, while I stayed in Salt Lake, tending to mom, he stayed in Park City. Sometimes, for weeks on end, we'd only saw each other for a few hours in the evening.

One night that stands out in my memory and obviously said something about his character, if I were listening, was when he came down to the farmhouse after work. Over dinner conversation, he told me about his business partner, a software engineer who wrote the code for their business's financial applications. A program the engineer wrote would ultimately be used by the whole financial services industry for pre-trade analysis, portfolio assessment, hedge assessments, and risk oversight. His partner, however, at the time, was being accused of stealing it from his in-laws, who were also software engineers and in the financial industry, as well.

The father-in-law had written a heartfelt letter to his daughter, the partner's wife, accusing her of abandoning her family and not doing the right thing by them. The letter and the charge had a very spiritual undertone about it as they were very devout Mormons. Blair, though, sat in the kitchen, relating the family conflict as if it were a funny anecdote, something to be amused by because it didn't affect him. I felt especially sorry for the father when Blair began poking fun and laughing at the father's spirituality. (RED FLAG) I found his remarks to be calloused and unfeeling.

After Blair's company began to grow and change, he said he needed capital to continue his business. He began to focus on my mother and other friends, and started grooming them to be investors. He knew my mother had done very well for herself, and had a very comfortable portfolio, so any chance he got, he'd talked up his company to her, telling her that she should invest, that his company was going to go public, and that a lot of friends stood to make a lot of money. My Mom, always the savvy investor in new products, was intrigued. After all, she had not become a millionaire by being afraid of a little risk. Now, I don't know if he intentionally set out to steal from her but desperate means call for desperate measures. And though I tried to talk her out of it, she decided to cash out her life insurance policy and invest in his company. Something did not feel right about the whole scheme. I was not a financial planner. I did not understand all the lingo but I knew intuitively that something was up. Maybe it was because I knew about the partner's family troubles and anticipated a lawsuit or perhaps, all those red flags were still waving in the breeze in my thoughts. I told Mom about my concerns, but she disagreed and invested $150,000 into his company anyway. A few months later, everything fell apart, and all I can say is, thank God, she did not invest the entire insurance payout.

As with all people who have both light and darkness in them, Blair had a very good, kind side. I believe he truly cared for my mom. When we heard of a church in San Francisco that had relics of a saint who was known to cure cancer, Blair made arrangement to fly us all there. He made reservations at one of the finer hotels and put my mom in the nicest room they had.

When we found the Church of St. John the Russian, we went in, kissed the relics, and said our prayers, asking for mom to be healed. We left San Francisco full of hope and making plans for the future. But Mom was weak and unsure if she could be healed. The most we could do, at that point, was hope for the best.

Unfortunately, it didn't work, and a few months, later she got weaker and weaker and became bed-ridden. It was heartbreaking to watch my once vibrant, confident, and headstrong mother become more of a sickly child. It seemed like an unnatural reversal of roles – me caring for her and her looking to me for help and comfort. I recognized, all too clearly, the need in my mother's eyes. It was the same need she undoubtedly saw in my eyes when she cared for me when I had the chicken pox as a child.

When winter came, my brother, sister, and I took turns taking care of her.

In the mornings, when I woke, if it had snowed, I would go out to scrape it off Blair's Land Rover and start it up so he could drive to up to Park City in a warm car. I would then walk over to my mom's house, give her her morning medications, try to feed her and - the worst part of all - inject her abdomen with morphine. I absolutely hated it! The morphine could only do so much to alleviate the pain of her cancer or the pain of her becoming a shadow of her former self. During this time, there was plenty of pain to go around and there was nothing that all the drugs in the world could about it.

By the end of the day, I was physically and emotionally exhausted. Then it was my sister's or brother's shift. One of them would come by to spend the night and relieve me of my caretaker duties. The hardest part of the whole day was when I had to say goodbye to my mother. I never knew if it would be my last, so I would linger for a while, unable to pull myself away from her bedside. I felt guilty for leaving but unable to stay, so with every kiss goodbye, with every thought unsaid, I left just a little piece of myself behind.

I lost my mother to cancer three years after my father died of the same, awful disease.

The evening I buried my mother, Blair and I had a terrible fight. I suppose, looking back, emotions were raw and it was not the best time to resolve relationship issues. And I don't fully remember how or why it all started. I remember Blair yelling at Jonathan for something he had done and Jonathan yelling back that Blair was nothing but a liar and a cheater. I was furious with Jonathan for disrespecting Blair in this way. Blair had always been good to the boys and I thought he deserved some recognition for that from them. When Jonathan stormed off, I followed him to his bedroom. I told him that he was to apologize to Blair, at once! Jonathan was so angry and upset that his eyes were slant and piercing. He blurted out that Blair's daughter had told him that her father was cheating on me with another woman, that he had cheated on her mother too, and the other woman in our marriage was a Princess, a philanthropist, and daughter of a famous movie star.

I rather stumbled out of Jonathan's room in a daze and found my way down the hall and to the living room to confront Blair. I was in shock. It felt as though the whole world was crumbling down around me – not unlike the awful feeling I had in my friend's bedroom just before the floor opened up to the pit of hell.

When I repeated to Blair what Jonathan had said, he denied it with such ferocity, such force that my heart sank. I knew that it was true. He threw his hands in the air as a gesture of defeat, grabbed his keys and said that he didn't *'want to listen to this shit anymore,'* and literally ran out of the house.

I followed him outside, screaming in both terror and disbelief. He ignored my grief. And without saying another word, he got in his Land Rover to leave, put the Rover in reverse and I, instinctively and stupidly, grabbed the front bumper, as if I could stop all of this from happening with my sheer will and strength. I begged him not to leave. But he continued to back up, pulling me along the snow covered graveled driveway. As he increased his speed, I could no longer hang on and my hands slipped off. I laid in the cold, icy dirt crying. He put the Rover in drive and left. I will never forget my knees scraping along the sharp little rocks in the dirty, cold snow and me, foolishly holding onto what I thought was happiness.

It was all just too much; caring for my mother as she lay dying, then learning the same day of her funeral that the wonderful man I had entrusted with my hopes and my heart was nothing more than a mirage – a trick of the mind. I was on the verge of a nervous breakdown, or perhaps I had slipped over the edge and had fallen directly into a morass. I no longer wanted to live. Nothing was real anymore and if it seemed real it was only going to make me hurt much worse later.

Of all the adversity I had been through in my life, Russell's suicide, my father's death, Christopher's hospitalization, my mother's death -- I had not given up hope. I had not given up on life. But this was different, I knew it, and it scared me. This time I had no angels whispering in my ear to choose sadness or happiness. I knew I was in trouble so I called my former therapist Marybeth, who had helped me with the emotional mess Russell left behind. I told her about everything that had happened and the devastation I felt inside, the feelings of rejection, worthlessness, and despair.

She admitted me to the hospital for observation and prescribed some anti-depressants. She considered me a suicide risk and, looking back, I suppose I was. Without a doubt, this whole episode – losing my mother, losing Blair, losing my sanity - was one of the worst experiences of my life. But the hardest thing of all was Christopher having to come to a psych ward to see his mother. He was so loving and gentle, and so worried that he was going to lose me after just losing his grandmother. He came daily and it tore my heart out to have to have him see me like that, his strong mother in such a weakened state. Chris was so loving and so sweet, but God, it was so awful!

My mother always told me to make sure to choose the right partner because it would determine the rest of your life. How right she was! I now had two totally disastrous marriages and no clue as to what I was doing wrong. I married for love both times not money, but clearly, I loved too many of the wrong people. I know now that there were red flags. I know now what it was they were warning me about (hindsight, in some ways, is an awful consequence of being sentient). But what I don't understand is why certain people don't come with warning labels tattooed on their foreheads. It would make mate selection so much easier. My instincts were intact; I had just failed to pay attention them.

I did not file for divorce right away and yet, all the while I was in the hospital, for two whole weeks, Blair did not come to visit me, not once. All the moments we shared, all the words of love, and all along his one true love, I believed, was money. He had left my arms and was now wrapped in avarice's embrace. Good for him, he found his treasure.

Though I was betrayed and devastated, I was, after all, warned and even told outright that I wasn't his type. And in his defense, he probably felt sorry for me, and only followed through with the marriage out of kindness, which sounded familiar. I eventually came to believe that the reason for our coming together in the first place, was to help my mother transition into her death. And for that, I will always be grateful.

Eventually, because we don't get there easily, I came to realize that by forgiving him, I was letting go of the hurt. And that, regardless of the way he went about it, he was where he needed to be, to experience his life the way *he* wanted to experience it. He was, and for all I know, is happy with his Princess, making his own choices, and creating his own life. Forgiving him gave me peace. And today, that is all I want or need.

I found great comfort looking inside myself and not blaming Blair. I was ready to criticize myself but the solution was found quickly. I humbled myself in the love of God and asked for His mercy. In this relationship, I found yet another blessing and it was not for me to judge him. Life is full of forces of darkness and light, and if we continue to reach for the light, no harm can come to us. If through suffering we help others to understand, we become more spiritually advanced. There are times when we are very sensitive to the remarks of our friends and loved ones and they seem unkind. However, if we go into ourselves deep enough, we find that it is us who are out of tune; we who have turned away from the light.

Kindred Spirits

Three years after my mother passed away, along with my marriage to Blair, I was back working in Park City, as a sales rep for Elegante, which sold beautiful home furnishings. Since I had an acumen for design and fashion, I was called on to consult on the occasional room or home design for my boss's clients.

At this time in my life, I was so discouraged by my ability, or lack thereof, to choose a good guy that I quit dating all together. I was really, more than okay with my celibacy and myself. Chris had recently joined the Air Force and Jonathan decided life with me was too crazy so he went to live with his father, and I didn't blame him. I had felt a strong pulling force towards a monastic life for many years and thought, perhaps now would be a good time to make my plans. I told my priest that I wanted to pursue the life of a nun once Jon turned eighteen years old.

One afternoon while I was working, two attractive men came into the store. They meandered around picking up items and talking in low voices. I watched as the tall, blonde one pick-up a fragrant candle and put it to his nose. The other, a man with definite Middle Eastern features – dark skin, dark eyes, and dark hair - wandered around, looking at other wares. After they'd exhausted their interest in the store's offerings, they approached the counter, setting a candle down to buy.

As I wrote up a receipt for sale, we chatted politely about one thing or another, undoubtedly the skiing conditions in Park City, which was the usual conversation with tourists. I wrapped the candle, put it in a small bag, and handed it to the blonde man. Before they left, the other man turned to me and said, "You know, you just sold a candle to Randall Wallace." I wasn't trying to be rude, but I had absolutely no clue who Randall Wallace was, and was sure they could see it in my expression. I felt kind of foolish and did not intend to be disrespectful, so I apologized, but then realized that an apology wasn't exactly in order either. I had not, after all, done anything wrong. Naively I asked, "So, I should know you - why?"

They both laughed. The dark-haired man, acting as his true fan, told me that the blond man was Randall Wallace the writer of *Braveheart* and directed *The Man in the Iron Mask* and other movies and T.V. programs. Randall stood humbly by while his friend sung his praises. Oh! How interesting, I thought. Not because I was impressed with him being a producer, writer, director and all the fame it brings but because *The Man in the Iron Mask* was one of my favorite movies. I am a sucker for happy endings (aren't we all?) and if the good guys prevail over evil, well they don't get any better than that. After the two were assured that I now knew who I had sold a candle to, they said goodbye, and I continued working the rest of my shift.

Shortly before quitting time, Randall came in again. This time he was alone and wasn't shopping. He came in the door, spotted me at the counter and came right over. I was surprised to see him and couldn't imagine what could have gone wrong with a candle. But he wasn't there to complain about the merchandise, he came to ask if I would join him and his friend for dinner after I got off work. I had nothing better to do so I told him I would. We agreed to meet at an Asian restaurant down on Main Street. There was an interesting attraction between us but it was not sexual. I just couldn't put my finger on it.

By the time I got to the restaurant, the two men were seated and waiting for me. Randall stood and held the chair for me as I sat down.

I thought of all the dates I had been on that I had to seat myself and thought, this is nice, chivalry isn't dead. I ordered a glass of wine and an appetizer and began to feel more comfortable on my first date in three years, even though it was with two men instead of one. During the dinner conversation, I shared with them my earnest desire to become a nun. I typically did not go around telling complete strangers my wish for a monastic life but there was something about the evening conversation that made it relevant. Of course, from the dark-haired friend, I got the usual comments about being too attractive to enter a convent and the remark that it would be a waste, as if the outside of a person was more important than what was inside. For some people, that's all they see and all that they understand. Randall however, just looked at me intently. I wasn't sure what the look meant but it put me at ease when he did not discount my idea as his friend had done.

After a couple of hours, I told them it was time for me to head home. I thanked them for dinner, put on my coat and got ready to leave. Randall, again the gentleman, walked me to my car. It was cold and it was snowing, which meant for another day of good skiing. We stood outside the car for a bit longer. He told me he was heading back to California but would like to see me again when he came back, if that was okay with me. I told him I'd be delighted and gave him my phone number.

A few weeks later he called. He was back in town and invited me to dinner and a movie with him and his dark-haired friend. He said that he and his friend were going to preview his new film *We Were Soldiers* at the friend's home movie theater. It sounded like a fun and interesting night.

The three of us met for dinner and then headed back to his friend's house in the hills above Salt Lake City. Coming up the drive, I marveled at how large the house was. When I walked in the front door, I was struck by how immaculate everything was -- and I mean *immaculate*. Everything from the floors, the doors, and the furniture shined with a high gloss. Our footsteps echoed in the foray and down the hallways while his friend gave us a tour of his home. I could see that he was quite pleased with his décor and couldn't help but think that he must have spent a small fortune on the rare hardwoods floors, and imported marble tile and counters. When he showed us his personal clothes closet, I thought that it would put any men's clothing store to shame. I mean, how can anyone know what they are going to wear when there are a million pieces to choose from, let alone which one they *want* to wear?!

The home movie theater was in a large room, with most of one wall a large television screen. The chairs were comfortable but not like what you would see in a theatre. Randall put the movie in the player. As the credits rolled and the score blared from the wall speakers, I could see he was in director mode. The movie kept my interest, up until the war images flashed across the screen. I did not want to be a killjoy but I had a hard time watching it. Though only a movie and the actors only playing a part, it was too close to the horror of real war. The thought that I was watching someone's son die and the suffering inflicted on others, was just too disturbing.

Christopher had joined the Air Force right out of high school. He had just gotten out of boot camp when 9/11 happened. The President had sent our boys to war and I explained to Randall that I wanted no visuals of boys being killed in battle. I had seen enough death in my life and it ran a bit too close to home for me. I shared with him how I had raced to F.E. Warren in Cheyenne Wyoming where Christopher was stationed in a pounding rain. I thought for sure and was scared to death that he would be sent off to war, but when I pulled up to the base, it was surrounded by giant tanks, bomb sniffing dogs, huge halogen lights, and machine guns that, I felt, were pointing squarely at me. They did let me on base to see my baby boy, now a man and off to war.

I was very touched that Randall completely understood. And I went out to sit on the patio while he and his friend watched the trailer. To this day, although it won several awards, I cannot watch that movie in its entirety. Christopher, however, thinks it's one of the best films ever made.

After the movie ended and I was saying my goodbyes, we made plans to meet for lunch at the Moroccan Hotel downtown in Salt Lake City before Randall went back to California.

It was the first time since we had met that we were alone. We sat in a booth and talked casually about ourselves. He brought the conversation full circle to the day of our first meeting. He wanted to know why I wanted to be a nun. He said, "You don't usually run into attractive women with a couple of kids who want such a drastic change in life."

"What shall I say?" I began. "How do you explain to someone the unexplainable? How, or even why try to convince someone else of something that is so deep within our heart and so precious that by trying to take it out and express it, would be to defile its beauty? Doing so would destroy its very nature. Besides oftentimes it only falls on deaf ears. Even people who have ears don't hear what is being shouted from heaven anyway!

"I will say this," I continued, "for at least the last five years or more I have desired to be a nun. It probably started when I found out that women who bore children could still become nuns. I asked the Abbot why someone would want to become a nun, and if my desire to become one could really be an escape from something."

"He told me that people try to escape from life in many ways; drugs, alcohol, relationships, depression, gambling, sex, etc. but rarely, if ever, do they consider monasticism. I assume people have a natural fear of God within them and I cannot imagine the Hell one would experience if they chose to follow God for any reason other than their heart called them to do so."

I told him that I was never encouraged to become a nun by anyone. It was only *my* true desire. And quite to the contrary, I had been discouraged, and even disbelieved, but it felt right for me.

"I believe in God," I said, "I believe in my Church. When I first started going to the convent in Brookline, I didn't know anyone. Then, after church one Sunday, a nun asked me to stay for lunch. I didn't even know that people could do that, that it was part of their service. She nodded encouragingly for me to stay so I accepted."

I related to Randall how I ended up sitting at a long table with the nuns, the table for the other lay people was full. And as we stood after the lunch was over and said prayers, my gaze turned towards the window and heavenward.

"That day," I emphasized, "that moment, I thanked God for letting me be in the presence of His earthly angels. Make no mistake, I will never consider myself worthy of such an honor, nor do I feel I'll ever become as sweet as they are. My desire to become a nun is solely based on the fact that I LOVE GOD with in every fiber of my being that is not dead from passions and despondency. I truly believe I will be closer to my God by choosing the life of a nun. I only pray God will find me worthy enough to live that kind of life someday."

I told him that I had tried to date again after two years of abstinence, and even dated the brother of one of the nuns. The day we met for our first date, I was standing in the convent living room, waiting for him to arrive, and asked whichever spiritual angel happened to be around to answer my question, 'Should I date?' I said aloud and turned to the bookshelf, opened a book from Saint Theophan the Recluse, and pointed my finger to a paragraph that contained the following passage:

Monasticism itself is a perpetual labor of conquering the passions and uprooting them in order that one may preserve oneself before the face of God in a pure and immaculate state. This, then, is your task! Give attention to it, and direct all your powers toward it.

It couldn't have been any clearer; glory to God for my answer, glory to God for all things, and glory to God for bringing me to this church!

I then told Randall about Father Isaac, the monk who healed my son and other miracles I had witnessed, that there were things that had happened in my life that brought me to a faith I hadn't known before. I was pleased when he did not make light of my experiences or my beliefs. In fact, he seemed to share them to a certain extent. He told me that when he was young he wanted to be a minister and had attended divinity school. I felt very comfortable with him and then knew why; we were very similar in our views and values.

I had come to know, after doing so much spiritual work that connections are made frequently as we move through life. People show up in people's lives to learn or hear something that will help them here, there, now or later. It doesn't matter when, it matters who.

When he started to tell me about his wife, the feelings he had for her became apparent. He said they were in the midst of a divorce, but he still loved her very much. She was a ballerina and he reminisced about how much joy he received from watching her dance. He described her every movement as rhythmic and graceful. As he talked on about her, his eyes filled with tears. I could feel his heart breaking and wished that there was something I could do to ease his suffering. But the truth was, when it came to affairs of the heart, I couldn't avoid the agony of my own failed relationships so what could I possibly offer? How could I help him avoid his? I did my best and got a sense that whatever I told him seemed to console him and make him feel better.

I was relieved when the conversation shifted from his wife to his dear friend Mel Gibson. He said Gibson was a very religious man and was working on making a movie about Christ. He talked in general terms about their relationship and the movie. I listened intently and was quite interested in hearing more about it. The movie, *The Passion of the Christ*, came out two years later. I thought the movie was as shocking and disturbing as any war movie I had ever seen. I walked out of the theater, horrified! Whatever Gibson's faith taught him about Jesus Christ was certainly not mine. It was just too bad that I didn't offer to be a consultant on the movie when Randall told me about it. I could have done a better job for Christianity. Though it did, I suppose, get people who loved blood and guts to recognize Christ – albeit, Hollywood style.

When our lunch ended a couple of hours later, I gave him a hug and said, goodbye. That was the last time I spoke with Randall but I will always consider him a seeker of peace.

Loss of Another Kind

My mother, though coming from a small mountain village, became quite a smart and skilled business woman. She had amassed well over a million dollars in diversified portfolios in two trust funds, stocks, bonds, and monthly income from one of her real estate buildings. She had her longtime friend, painstakingly arranged her assets and estate so that we would not owe a dime in inheritance taxes. With the exception of her Audi car payment, *she owned everything, free and clear*, and when she died, she left her estate in perfect order for us children.

My brother was named executor of my mother's estate, and within a week of Mom's death, decided we should restructure the assets and put them into a limited liability company (LLC). When we signed the papers to turn the Trust into an LLC, Mom's accountant told us that he respected my mother so much, that if we ever fought over the estate, he would resign immediately.

After the papers were signed, my brother started making some rather, well let's just say, questionable financial purchases, and he wanted me to start paying rent on my farmhouse. Mom had left her estate set up so that each of us would receive a small monthly income from the estate, *not* pay the estate. It occurred to me afterward, but not at the time, that my brother did not know about the arrangement I made with my parents. I thought that because Dad said I could buy it, and because I had made improvements and payments on the farmhouse, that it was someday going to be mine.

This was at a time when I had just been released from the hospital and was on strong antidepressants and anxiety medication. In retrospect, I was in no condition to be making financial decisions of that magnitude. If I wasn't in such a weakened state, I probably would have sought the advice of an attorney sooner than I did.

My brother, as part of his fiduciary responsibility, was providing statements to my sister and me. The statements listed everything he was spending but we never saw the actual bills. When I began regaining my footing and was better able to follow the numbers, I contacted my mother's lawyer. The numbers just did not add up and I wanted to know if I was possibly doing something wrong. After some research, the attorney said my brother was not exactly being fair in rationing the estate funds, so, on learning this, I brought my sister into the attorney's office to show her the changes that needed to be made to get a fair and equitable split of the estate. At that point, let's just say it got **_UGLY_**.

The showdown brewing, I told my brother that he could keep the entire estate, that I didn't care, and all I wanted was my farm, my sister and he could keep the rest. He refused. He had designs on my farmhouse property and would not let me have it. He wanted to subdivide the property for development, to have houses built on the property and make more money – exactly what the old man who sold my mother the farm did not want. What my brother told my sister was that he didn't have the money to buy me out, so she would have to put up her own home to pay me. In the end, my sister would not choose sides and wanted no part of the dispute, so rather than fight over the inheritance, which my mother would have hated, I relented. I surrendered the 'La La Land' farm to the estate, packed my bags and went back to Boston to live.

A few years later, my sister learned that what I had been trying to tell her was true and that my brother had been manipulating information. After that, they parted ways as well. But thank God, we eventually worked it all out and kept the family intact. It was touch-and-go for a while, but losing family over money is never worth it.

I had try to train myself in forgiveness and this would be no different, but it took a little longer to get there. Some nights, the devil would come back and haunt my thoughts. I would think and become upset about the greed of man. My brother had the farm home, and all I had left were the memories and a box of photos from that lovely place. The farm was not only a place, a piece of land, it was part of my family. It was where I had planted trees when my sons were born. It was where I taught them to ride a snowmobile. I spent many days watching them run around, chasing the lamb, the potbelly pig, and my adorable cute white ducks – Dally and Dolly.

It was a place of learning and growing for me and my boys. They climbed the fence to look at and pet the horses, just like I did as a child. It is where I taught Jonathan to hit a baseball off a 'T-ball' stand while still in diapers. It was where Christopher had his 8th birthday party after building a treehouse to host it in.

It was where my uncle brought me lambs to raise as newborns. Their mother had disowned them so I bottle fed them and named them Isaac and Abraham. Abraham, too weak from the beginning, died in my arms, and he, along with many other pets over the years, were buried on the property – their home and grave. I had hand-dug flower beds with my sons and painted murals on the entryway walls. We made ponds and made the farm our paradise. All our friends called it 'La-La Land.' That is how I will always remember it.

A few years later, after I had given in rather than cause a permanent family riff, my brother sold it for more than I received from the entire estate. Though he might have profited, I believe the land was cursed because the original agreement between my mother and the old man had been irretrievably broken. After my brother sold it, it was bought and sold four or five times to different developers. For reasons unknown, they were never able to have their plans come to fruition. The toys from my boys play lay around, untouched, unmoved. The murals we painted on the walls faded with time and became ghosts of what they had once been. For nearly 13 years the property sat deserted and vacant. Oddly, as I was planning to go to press with my book, the alternate vision for the property was realized. Houses and manicured lawns now sit atop a life I had once cherished and built. For me, life had become a constant 'letting go.' So why should I be surprised that this was any different?

From early in my youth, I watched as my Mom helped her brothers and sisters who were less fortunate. She was my guide, my compass, as to how I should treat others. I was again surprised when some 12 years later after she was gone, I got a phone call from her little brother, my Uncle Ernie. He said he was in a bind and needed my help, financially. I told him I would see what I could do. I called my sister and told her that Uncle Ernie needed us. I went on to tell her that I would be able to give him $500, and if she could give him $500 and Roy was willing to chip in, we could help the ol' man out. I fully expected that since she had ended up with the majority of what was left of mom's estate, she would have no concerns about my request. To my chagrin, she said she couldn't contribute the $500 because she was in the midst of getting all her stuff ready to go, to live in Italy for a year. She had been offered a home to stay in for free and a free trip to Rome but couldn't afford a pittance for her uncle. I couldn't believe it! But what really hurt me, was that she had become so hardened by all her money and her travel that she wouldn't, not that she couldn't, help her poor Uncle Ernie. After getting very upset, I came back to my center and thought, she can choose to do whatever she wants. I should not judge her behavior; she has her own reasons. And we are all the creators of our lives and her not wanting to help was just as valid as me wanting to help.

Once again, as with Blair, Russell, my brother, sister, and others, I had to let go. It was my path to forgiveness. People do have choices and free will to live their lives in the fashion they choose to live them. We are the co-creators of our lives.

Dilly, Dally, and Grunt on the farm

My chapel on the farm

My horse Blackie

My lamb Izzy

Chris and Jonathan on our little farm

Chris enlisted in the Air Force shortly after my mom died

Chapter 9: Birth of a Notion

Do not neglect to show hospitality to strangers, for thereby some have entertained angels unawares. - Hebrews 13:2

Kicking the Habit

It was my 50th birthday present to myself. Jonathan was going to be eighteen years old in two short years and I had decided that if I was going to be a nun, it would be a good idea to live in a monastery for a while, just to see if it was all I thought it would be. I called my sweet friend and abbess at the Convent of the Meeting of the Lord in Stanwood, Washington, and made arrangements to stay for a month.

It was quiet, beautiful, peaceful, and everything I hoped for and more, and if everything worked out the way I hoped, I would return as a novice once Jonathan was of age to be out on his own in the world.

Everyone at a convent has a job and chores to do and my job was working in the gardens, which were beautiful and the task suited me perfectly. I had been there only a few short weeks and was truly enjoying my stay, when I got a frantic phone call from Jonathan. He had been staying with his father in Boston and attending high school in Mashpee, Massachusetts.

"Mom, I just got home from school and my dad told me to go check on Bob. I went in there and, Mom -- *Bob's dead*. What should I do?"

"What? Bob's dead?! How do you know?" I stammered.

"Dad said Bob didn't feel well this morning when I left for school and he never came out of his room. Mom, he's just not breathing."

"Jonathan, call 911. Does your dad know?"

"I think -- I don't know!"

"Jonathan, hang up right now, go get your dad and tell him to call 911."

"Okay, Mom, I'll call you back."

About a half hour later, I called Jonathan back.

"Mom the paramedics and police are here. They are questioning Dad. I'll call you back."

Another hour passed. Jonathan called again with a status report.

"Well the police are trying to figure out who Bob really is."

"WHAT?! Who Bob *really is*!"

"I guess Bob isn't his real name," Jonathan continued. "Dad's friend from Europe called and asked if he could stay with Dad. He was on some sort of special assignment. Apparently, the guy works…or worked for the NSA."

"Are you kidding me?"

"Nope."

"And your dad doesn't know his real name? Oh God, Jonathan! Are you alright?"

"Yep. It's a little weird, that's all. I think, they think, Dad knows more than he does about the man."

"Okay, call me when you know more," and I hung up.

I went in and told the Abbess about what was happening and then I went into the chapel to light a candle for all three of them. My immediate instinct was to book the first flight to Boston to get Jonathan out of harm's way, if that was the case, and then another thought took hold of my situation.

I returned to the Abbess and said, "Mother Thecla, what if Jon had called to say he had been in a bad accident? If I were a nun would I be allowed to go to him?"

She smiled and waited a few minutes before her reply. "No," she said thoughtfully.

"Really?" I said. "What if he was dying?"

Once again, she hesitated while she weighed her response.

"You would have to get permission from the Elder, but I don't think he would let you go. We live a cloistered life here. We pray for those we love. There is no greater thing we can do for our loved ones,' she instructed me calmly.

Well that pretty much made up my mind for me. I guess, all those years of yearning to become a nun had just ended with the knowledge that I would not be free to help my boys if they needed me. I went back to my room and realized, I had gone there to get answers, and *I got them*. It seemed to me that Maria von Trapp and I had a lot in common. We were both taken away from the convent life by kids and captains (more on that later).

I spoke with Jimmy later that evening. He told me that Bob, as it turns out, was an operative in the NSA and really high-up on the food chain there. He pieced together a story about Bob and his friendship with a countess from some European country, who had been married to a man, who had been assassinated, and something about gold bullion that had been stolen during WWII. Clearly, I was too upset to pay attention to the details and it was also clear that the details were fuzzy to Jimmy too – on purpose. I wrote it off as Jimmy reading way too many spy novels.

I finished my visit with the nuns and returned to Boston, I checked in with Jonathan, who was doing just fine, all things considered. I think the whole episode was probably like last year's news to him. The only thing occupying his mind was his plan to participate in a talent show at school.

Finally Home

Years before my parents died, when I was living in Boston and the boys were little, I would take them on Sunday drives. I found an area that was breathtakingly beautiful. The towns I liked most were on the south shore – Hingham, Cohasset, and Scituate. One day, during one of our drives, I saw a large statue of the Madonna in the town square in Scituate. I stopped the car and prayed that she would help me find a house there someday. But after I looked at house prices, I knew that there was absolutely no way I could afford to live there. If it was going to happen, it would have to be divine intervention.

Years later, with the remainder of my inheritance from my mother's estate sitting in the bank, I was ready to purchase a home of my own. I went back to the south shore I loved so much and, just for fun, wanted to see if I could afford anything. I was quite surprised to find a twenty-room Victorian for only $350,000. I had a little under that from mom's estate so I felt I could invest it all into this house and my house payments would be affordable.

The way I found it, Jonathan and I were driving around the town of Hull, Massachusetts, on Boston's south shore, and stopped at a Real Estate office near the oceanfront. The waves that day were huge and just beautiful crashing against the shore. The realtors told me to drive around to some that were on the market, and if I saw one I wanted to look at, to let them know and they would arrange it.

The house was on a little peninsula and the first time I saw it I knew it was way more than what I was looking for. It was big. I mean, hotel-size big! Mansion big! The Atlantic Ocean was in the front yard and Hingham Bay in the back yard. I was instantly reminded of the line "water, water, everywhere" from Coleridge's *Rime of the Ancient Mariner*. I had prayed for water, and I got water.

As we pulled off the street into a large parking lot, we both looked up at an enormous house with a *For Sale* sign in the front yard. I couldn't believe it was a single-family home; it looked more like a hotel. I loved it the minute I saw it and knew it was going to be mine. I was so engrossed in our find that I didn't notice a woman, dressed in a silver fur-lined parka, walk in front of the car.

"Shit!" Jon said, "You almost hit that lady!"

I stopped the car – before hitting her – and she just smiled at me. She was in her late 40s - tall, blond, and beautiful. I rolled down the window and asked if she knew anything about the house for sale. She said her husband's family owned it and that they were having an open house that next weekend, and that I should come by to look at it then. I told her I would and said, goodbye. I didn't know, at the time, that she was living in the house. As we drove off, back to Boston, I told my son, "She is going to be a dear friend!" I just felt it.

I arranged a showing the following week. As I walked through this monster of a home with Jonathan, there was a beautiful little girl sitting at her computer and the owner and her friend were sitting in the great room playing with a cockatiel.

A month later it was mine.

Moving into my big, beautiful home was one of the most special feelings I had ever had. There was something so satisfying, so rewarding, so surreal about my lifelong dream coming true. With the key in hand, my eyes could see it was real. My fingers wrapped around the staircase banister could feel the solid wood in their grip. The echo of my footsteps resounded in my ears. But my heart and mind couldn't believe that this house was mine - all twenty rooms of it! For days, as I moved in boxes and furniture, I would stop, look around, and smile. 'It's mine,' was a refrain that played through my thoughts over and over again.

The first night I slept in my new bedroom, I opened a window that faced the ocean. I was instantly transported back to the nights back in Utah when I would hear the sound of the cars and traffic, imagining that it was the ocean and the waves rocking me to sleep. I now had the real thing! I somehow had created my dream home through my thoughts.

History and Mystery

Now that I owned this mansion and had settled in, it was time to learn a little bit more about my home. Sometimes, people would stop by and tell me stories about the house. Some people had lived there as a child or had family or friends who did. I learned the house was built in 1856 by Captain Asa Ransom, a Boston seafaring man, and his wife, Sara. After he retired, they built the Sagamore Hotel on Nantasket Beach in Hull.

Jonathan and I were always scouting around and investigating all the cracks and crevices of the house when we found, what can only be described as a collapsed tunnel in the basement on the beach side of the property. As with all very old houses, there were plenty of stories about it and its history. The story I found most intriguing, courtesy of the locals, given the find in the basement, was that the house had been used as a relay point for alcohol smugglers or 'rum runner' during the Prohibition era. Presumably, the boats would anchor off the beach and unload their illegal rum and gin, and under the cover of darkness, would use the tunnel to bring the booze into the basement, sight unseen. Adding a little plausibility to the story, was the fact that Joseph P. Kennedy, Sr. had a summer home in Hull and was said to have been friends with the owner of my house at the time. The implication of their friendship during this era was that they were in business together and stored their contraband alcohol in the basement of my house. It was a charming, interesting story but I did not give it much credence. The way I saw it, if you went anywhere near the coast of Massachusetts and *didn't* hear a tale about bootleggers, booze, and the Kennedys, you were probably in the wrong Massachusetts.

One evening, a friend, who had stopped in a local pub for a drink, met an elderly fisherman sitting at the bar. He got to talking with the old man and mentioned that I had just bought this large, historic home on the peninsula. After my friend described the house, the fisherman said he was very familiar with it. In fact, he had been inside the house when he as a very young boy. Then, with a bemused smile, he asked if we had found the hidden rooms in the basement. He added that there had once been a tunnel that was dug underneath the front porch that lead towards the ocean, but had since caved in.

Armed with this new bit of information, Jonathan and my interests in exploring the basement was renewed. We joked about what treasures the hidden rooms held in store for us - perhaps a long-forgotten crate of bootlegger's rum - which would have aged quite nicely by then. Or a room full of ancient coins, diamond encrusted baubles, and other precious objects, hidden there by pirates of the high seas. Or maybe we would stumble upon a laboratory, pronounced *'la·bor·a·tory'* by the mad scientist who once toiled in secret over beakers and test tubes, like an alchemist trying to turn base metals into gold. We felt as though we were on an adventure.

The basement had not been updated since the house was built. It had a dirt floor that filled the air with the smell of earth. It was about 1200 square feet with a hand-built stone foundation. We could see where the stones gave way and tumbled to the floor where the 'tunnel' had once been. Jutting out of the wall was an old coal chute used in the early 1900s to provide fuel for a monster-size coal burning furnace. Though we examined every inch of the basement for concealed openings and clandestine doorways, we couldn't find any evidence of hidden rooms. And, though, we may not have found any secrets of the old house, we sure had a lot of fun trying.

A few years later, with the hunt for hidden spaces well forgotten, Jonathan and I were in the basement looking for his surf board. Out of curiosity, he asked what I thought was behind a big piece of wood with an electrical cable bolted to it and nailed to the foundation and the rafters. I told him that I had no idea, that I had never thought about it, actually. But remembering the stories and our search for hidden rooms, I thought it was worth investigating. We found a hammer and a crowbar and began carefully pulling back the wood. There was, after all, an electrical cable attached to it and, possibly, creepy, crawly spiders behind it. To our delight and surprise—*there was a crawl space*! To where, we didn't know. I ran upstairs and called my handyman, Paul, and told him to come check it out immediately.

Flashlight in hand, Paul climbed into the opening we'd found. He scooted in about five or six feet until he came to a drop off, a drop off into a 10-foot by 10-foot stone covered room. Fortunately, the ceiling was about 7 feet high, high enough for him to stand. In the circle of light emitting from his flashlight, he found an old canvas legging from a WWI soldier's boot, a few old bottles, a lot of dead spiders, and, to his dismay, the carcass of a cat. There was no bootlegger's rum, no pirate's treasure, and no alchemist's gold. Just a bottle without the booze, a boot legging without a foot, and a poor creature without an escape. I chose not to crawl up into that hidden room. It now seemed just too eerie and creepy. And, after finding our morbid little cache, I was just as glad that we never found another room like it.

Tools of my Trade

I was becoming fond of my new old home and decided to take an evening job nearby so I could work on it during the day. I found a job nearby at the Square Café as a waitress.

I loved to decorate and my twenty-room Victorian gave me plenty of opportunity to be creative and to make each room a masterpiece. Since I had put all my money into buying the house, I was revenue challenged when it came to the renovations. I needed to be as creative about my budget as I was about my design. Oftentimes, the colors of the rooms weren't determined by any particular artistic vision but by the paint mistakes sitting on the $5.00 table at the Home Depot or Lowes. I painted the floors that couldn't be restored with large squares and stenciled them with appealing designs. I used joint compound to stucco over ugly wallpaper that proved too hard to remove. I did a faux stone wall in what I called, the 'Great Room' using National Geographic as my template for the size of the stones. My imagination and my life were unleashed in a very good way.

All my spare time was spent on the house, as well as some of the spare time of my friends. It was not only my home, it was my ultimate project. I felt as though I was exactly *where* I was meant to be exactly *when* I was supposed to be there. Life was still a challenge at times, but it always is anyway, as long as you're still alive and breathing.

When I needed a break from the work, I would take the ferry over to Boston and spend the day away from what my friends and I jokingly called "Gilligan's Island" in Hull. It had come to be called that because my friends in Hull, who had become so dear to me, rarely left the little town. And, carrying the analogy a little further, I dubbed my best friend Sally was 'Mary Ann,' and my handyman, Paul, was 'Gilligan.' Sally's husband, George, who ran the local diner, was the 'Skipper.' It became a running joke amongst us whenever I would head over to Boston to the 'mainland.' Jonathan and I, however, did not qualify for a Gilligan's Island nickname because we had transportation off the 'Island,' or I suppose I would have been 'Ginger.' Sally's husband wouldn't let her use their old, beat-up minivan and Paul had lost his driver's license due to too many DUIs.

My home restoration took many hours, days, months, and years. Most all of it was done primarily by myself, with the occasional help of 'Gilligan,' who only charged me twenty-five bucks an hour!

When I needed extra help with the grounds in the summer, I would hire homeless veterans to do some landscaping, digging ponds, moving dirt, trimming hedges, or mowing the lawn. I was grateful for their service and think they were glad to be working. I suppose word got out that I hired help when a big, brawny, bald man with a terrible looking scar on his head walked by the house one day, stopped and asked if I would hire him. He said he would work for whatever I could pay, which wasn't much. I had been digging up a huge area of the backyard for a patio and really needed the help so I hired him. His speech was a bit sluggish and he appeared to be a little slow-minded but he worked very hard, which was all I needed from him. 'Gilligan' called him 'Half-brain' and he didn't seem to mind.

After he had been working for me for a while, he told me that he got the scar on his head from falling off a ladder while he was working on a roof. That, I thought, could explain a lot. He also confided that he had just gotten out of prison, for what, I didn't know. But I believed, and still do, in giving people the benefit of the doubt and an opportunity to show they've changed, so I wasn't concerned about that part of the man's past. He was very respectful and helpful. That's what mattered. Until one day when I found his name on the sex offenders registry for our neighborhood. Since Jonathan was still a bit young, that, for me, was a deal breaker. After that I always said I didn't need any help if he asked for more work after that. He never came around after a while. He just kind of disappeared. Then, a couple of years later, there was a knock at the door. I was right in the middle of a project so Jonathan answered the door. I heard Jonathan tell the visitor, I was not available. Then I heard a man say, "Your mother hired me once, and really helped me out. I was just in the area and wanted to say, hello, and thank her again for helping me during such a bad time."

Jonathan assured him that I would get the message. As he walked off the porch, he paused and yelled back to my son, "Hey man, you have a really, really kind mom! Tell her, 'thanks!'"

Sally, Oh Sally

My friend, Sally, is precious.

Sally was a tremendous help when I moved in. I was new to the area so she gave me the lay of the land as it were. She told me where the Town Hall was and where to do my shopping.

She and her husband, George, owned and operated the diner next door. I would go to the Corner Café to get my meals as I worked day and night to get the house move-in ready. If she wasn't waitressing, she could be found sitting at the counter with a crossword puzzle in front of her or looking at an atlas to see where some of her customers hailed from.

If I were ever a contestant on a game show like *Cash Cab*, where people answer questions for cash, she would be my *shout-out* call, when you need help with an answer. She was, and *is* that smart! The men who hung out on the boardwalk once told me that, years earlier, every man in Hull considered her the most beautiful woman on the South Shore. And she was, both inside and out. To this day, I have never heard her say a bad word about anyone, and trust me, in the town of Hull, there was plenty to say!

George was a typical Greek husband; demanding, occasionally selfish towards his family, but generous to others. Coming from Greek heritage, I recognized the cultural traits and, sometimes, they weren't pretty. He loved old music and had an infectious laugh. He could be unpredictable and explosive. He would be really sweet while he was cooking, insisting that you to try his freshly made meals, which were often pulled together from his own recipes, then, moments later, he could erupt and scream at Sally from the kitchen about something that was bugging him, which he didn't seem to notice bothered his customers or his wife.

After I got the home in livable condition, on the advice of my friend, Rod, who was a successful developer in Utah, I made several rooms on the second floor into a rentable in-law apartment. And, thank God, I did. The rent often helped me keep up on the mortgage payments. It was really quite spacious with three bedrooms, one serving as the living room, a bath, and a kitchen. My first renters were two men from Florida who were in the area working on the nuclear power plant in Quincy. The short-term housing that I provided suited their needs and mine.

Occasionally, the men would have their wives come to stay, which was fine with me. I never minded the extra company and I would often sit with them on the porch and chat with them about their lives, the weather, high and low tides, and everything in between. One particular weekend, one of the wives came to stay while her husband went to work. We were sitting on the deck, chatting about the church they attended in Florida when Sally walked up, dropped down in one of the deck chairs, and lit up a cigarette. She had just returned from her annual Memorial Day weekend-get-away in Provincetown, Massachusetts with George. I could feel her high energy as she took a few puffs of her cigarette and she began to speak.

"Ohhh muy Gawd! Men! Men!" she said and shook her head in disgust.

"Here I spend all summer long working my butt off dealing with tourists," she continued, "saving my tip money so that I can get books to read on my weekend off, laying on the beach in the sun, in peace and quiet. My feet get raw and sore from standing on them all day long and they need a rest! I need a rest, perhaps even a foot massage. But, noooo...there I am, comfortably reading a great book in my beach chair when George—ohhh muy gawd—George!" she shook her head again and took another drag from her cigarette.

"That's my husband," she told the girl who was a total stranger to her, as if the surprise on her face communicated a need for clarification.

"George comes up to me with two bicycles. 'Come on, Sally, let's go for a bike-ride,' he says. Now, you think I wannah go for a bike ride? Of course not! The last thing my legs or I want to do is to start peddling in the sand dunes!"

At that Sally stood up and pantomimed peddling as if she were riding a bike. Her long, tan legs moved up and down as though every pump of the pedal was an extreme effort. Her hands gripped the invisible handlebars and she huffed and puffed with the cigarette still dangling from her mouth. She told us how she was trying to keep up with her husband, and cussed him under her breath for taking her away from her book, the sunshine and her happy place.

She said, as she came up over a knoll, she couldn't see him anymore but peddled on hoping to catch up with him soon. Her legs were killing her, her butt was sore from the seat of the bike and she was sweating like a wet dishrag just trying to make it over the hill. Then, from a tall grassy spot on the beach, she heard George call her name.

"Sally! Come ovah heah!" he shouted.

She put the imaginary bike down, stood straight up and looked at us.

"Do you know what he was doing? Do ya wanna guess what he was doing?!" her voice reaching a crescendo as she leaned into us. Then in a low, deeper voice said; "He is laying there with his pants pulled down around his ankles and has the nerve to tell me to come over there and ride 'Big Daddy.' Can you believe he did that?! Big Daddy!!! As if the bike ride wasn't painful enough!"

We laughed so hard, we had tears streaming down our faces. The mortified expression on her face made us laugh all the harder. I was laughing so hard, I think I may have even wet myself. To this day, whenever I think of her story and her dramatization, I can't help but chuckle.

Sally and I soon became uber-amigos, split-a-parts, two sisters from different mothers. She would come over and we would discuss our children, our spouses, our friends, our meals and our spiritual lives. She was raised in the Vedic tradition and I had joined the Orthodox Church; different faiths but both had love as their essence.

Our connection was uncanny. We would go days without seeing each other. Then, when we did see each other, we'd find out that we had been sick at the same time. And though this is not unusual if it happens once, or even twice, but it happened all the time. It became something that, if we didn't see each other, we would check our own lives to know why.

We often discussed our children like most mothers' do. She had two beautiful girls. The younger one, Gina, would sometimes play in my garden, catching baby snakes to feed to her cat. She was the same age as my son, Jonathan, so they would play together at my house or hers. Jonathan, at that time, was a bit overweight. I was concerned that the other children in the neighborhood and at school would make fun of him, like I endured when I was young. But Gina always treated him with respect and made him feel right at home and I appreciated that.

Sometimes we would talk about what was going on in the town and what people were up to. But mostly, we talked about George, and mostly on Mondays. The Corner Café was closed on Mondays and he would go over the bills and the budget and then go off to the food market. Sally would come over to hide from him. After he went over the business finances, he would get pissed off because he wasn't making enough money. If Sally wasn't hiding at my house, he would go on a tirade and go on-and-on about how they were going to lose their business and their house. It was very hard for her to feel happy and secure in her life when she lived with George 'Chicken Little' Anastos.

The thing that was so irritating about listening to the money shortage issue was that George was an avid gambler. He could often be found pouring over the *Racing News*, picking horses for up-coming races. I don't think he won a lot and don't think he played to win. I think he just wanted to pick the horse, jockey, and trainer in different combinations. I have no idea what he got out of it but it sure as hell wasn't money.

Sally, oh how she could make me laugh!

On most evenings, after the diner closed, you could find Sally and me, her with her vodka and cranberry juice and me and my wine, laughing hysterically about one thing or another. Sometimes we would listen to old albums and start dancing on the lawn. Other times, on hot summer nights, she would sleep with her two girls on the deck overlooking the marina on a mattress they pulled from the house.

One night, I went up to join her. She lay on the mattress, looking at the stars. I lay down next to her, then, out of the blue and for whatever reason, we started singing songs from the old movie musicals - from *Singing in the Rain* to *Mary Poppins* to *The Sound of*

Music. We didn't know all the words to *The Sound of Music,* so I would sing '...the hills are alive...' and she would sing the chorus, way off key, '.... Ahhhh –Ah- Ah- Ahhhhh.' Then we would giggle ourselves crazy like little girls. The only way you can have that much fun with another person is to come from the same place in the heart. And we did. We were true little girls when we were together.

The Doc

Most mornings, I would take my morning cup of coffee and walk across the street to Nantasket Beach so that I could wake up with the sun. I loved to feel the cool sand and the sea between my toes. The sun rose in the east and called to me between the hours of five and six to say 'good morning' to God, and thank Him for all my blessings.

Watching the sliver of sun rise from below the horizon, splashing its light on the waves made me feel as though all the angels in heaven had summoned me there. It was a peaceful, empowering way to start the day. My morning ritual made it easy to wake up. I was as eager as a child on Christmas morning to get up and go meet the day and unwrap the presents waiting for me. It was important for me to be one of the first people at the seashore, with my cup of coffee in one hand and my beach chair in the other. It was important that I get there by sunrise. Otherwise, hordes of people would fill the beach with bodies, towels, umbrellas, radios, coconut smelling suntan oils, which didn't go well with my coffee, and their strong, thick, Bostonian accents.

Occasionally, I would run into my old friend, 'The Doc,' as he called himself. He was an elderly man who lived on Hingham Point, a few miles away. His circulation was poor so he tried to walk in the mornings to maintain his health. He seemed rather frail and I sensed his health was failing, but he was always spunky, friendly, warm and generous. He had told me during one of our conversations that he had been on many beaches, all around the world but none were quite as magical as this one. I had not been to many beaches myself so who was I to disagree?

During our mornings together, we would walk the beach and talk about the town, about the corruption in the world, and about the corruption of the medical industry, which was his former business hence the moniker 'The Doc.' When I met him, he had been retired and was disgusted with, what he believed, were the evil doings of the medical world. He never really talked about his role in the industry and I don't know if he was actually a doctor, a hospital administrator, or someone who worked with medical insurance. All I know is that he devoted his life to something that now caused him disappointment and pain, which must be the saddest regret of all - to spend your life in the service of something that ultimately is not worthy of your time and soul. My heart ached for him.

One morning, while we squished the sand between our toes, we listened to Frank Sinatra blaring from his car radio parked up on the boardwalk, and stared at the clear cold salty water. I shared with him my desire to someday become a nun. He just snickered. He asked me where I lived. I pointed to my old Victorian home – of which I was so proud - across the street and told him everything I had done to renovate it. I'm sure he could see what my home meant to me.

He asked, "What is the room up there in the cupola?"

Jokingly, I said, "Oh, my tower? That's where I'll write my book." Though I kept a journal, I never really thought seriously about writing a book - well, maybe, in the deep recesses of my mind.

"What are you going to write about?" he asked.

I told him about my idea about writing a memoir. I told him about the things that I had experienced in my life. I told him, about my visions, my heartaches, and my view of life, love, and God. He listened intently. Then, surprising to me, he gave me a big, heartfelt hug.

"My dear," he said, "do you have an agent or a publisher, yet?"

Laughing at the thought that I had something someone would want to read, I said in a kind of teenage tone in response to did-you-do-your-homework, "Nooo."

He continued looking up at the tower. Then, with an undecipherable smile he said, "It's going to be a wonderful book then."

"How do you know?" I said.

"Because," he responded, "you are going to write it from your heart. And, after days of talking, and walking with you, I can tell, you have a big one!" At that point, he handed me his business card. He told me that his daughter was a producer for a television network.

We talked about his wife, who was a local stage actress and the aunt or sister of either Doris Roberts, who played Ray Romano's mother on the T.V. series *Everybody Loves Raymond*, or, maybe Ray's real mother, I never really bothered to find out which one.

The Doc loved his wife and spoke about her often; how beautiful and talented she was, how much he adored her, and how hard he thought it must have been for her living with him. Again, I could feel his regrets well up in him and my heart ached for him. Regret is an awful thing to live with because the situation around the regret can never be undone; there is no do-over. It is what it is and what it will always be, and that is with you until you learn to let it go.

It's been many years since I've seen The Doc. I think of him often. During one of our morning meetings, he gave me a gift. It was a very small medallion of the Virgin Mary, which I have to this day. When he gave it to me, I gave him a tiny stone I brought home with me from my visit to the Holy Land. That was the last day we saw each other. Funny that we shared gifts on that last meeting. After that, the summer turned warmer, my projects took more and more of my time, and I spent less and less time at the beach. Though I would still go to the beach in the mornings, he wouldn't be there. I supposed that he had moved away. He came into my life and then was gone.

I still think of him and our friendship whenever I go to the beach no matter where in the world I may be. I miss him to this day.

An Inn is Born

My sister and her friends descended upon my new home one weekend. She usually travels with an entourage with partying as the top priority, to Golf, to go fly fishing or fishing of any kind. She lives to fish as well as to go to shit-kicking country bars; her mouth can make a truck driver blush and I find it fascinating how many men are drawn to her. She casts her net wide, and always reels one in when she travels. However, she is strictly catch and release. She certainly changed over the years from that shy, sweet, studious, little girl in school.

She owns a hair salon in Salt Lake City. Most of her clients are men. She regularly has two colors in her hair just like one of the many cowboy boots in her closet. She lives in a 1950s style rambler, and no one would never know that her husband and mother left her very well off. She changes clothes as frequently as she changes men, and like the clothes left around her home, so too, are the men scattered around the country.

She refers to them geographically such as Baltimore Mike, Texas Tim, Seattle Dave, Aspen Randy, or by occupation such as Cowboy Clyde, Farmer Greg, Longhair Ron, or Fisherman Phil. She flies around the country on a buddy pass given to her from a friend who works at Delta. He isn't a boyfriend but probably wants to be! She never plans where she is going or how long she will stay. She just picks up and goes with whomever wants to join her on her escapades or adventures, of which there are many, and which is why she usually has an entourage. She just decides to go and there is usually someone willing to follow.

She has a very sharp wit and is willing to try anything. Everywhere she goes has a story. Tombstone, Arizona for example where, one weekend, she and her side kick Lisa (the two of them traveled frequently together and were appropriately named 'Thelma and Louise') met two cowboys at a bar. The men were proving to be overly obnoxious so they slipped the nastier one part of a valium to calm him down. The guys wanted to party after the bar closed so my sister put them in the backseat of her convertible Saab. Then they stopped at a local store to pick up more beer and while the men were in the store, Thelma and Louise drove off, leaving two very confused, inebriated, hormone-exhilarated men standing alone on a deserted Arizona street in the wee hours.

On this particular trip she and five of her friends came from Utah to visit me at my 'new' old beach house in Hull. We were all sitting on the wraparound deck in our jammies and swimwear, sipping coffee and talking. They said I had a beautiful home and had done a wonderful job renovating it. Then, as these things happen, one of her friends suggested I make my house into an Inn, like a Bed and Breakfast or a B&B as it is known in the trade. I knew nothing about running an Inn. I thought about what it would be like to have strangers in and out of my house. But as the idea grew in my mind, I became more and more convinced that it was something that I wanted to do. Many days I would sit on my deck looking out at the ocean thinking it was a shame that I didn't have anyone to share it with. If you have something beautiful it should be shared.

So, I went to the local book store and bought a couple of books: *Bed and Breakfasts for Dummies* and *Starting a B&B for Beginners*. I followed some of the suggestions, and skipped the ones I couldn't relate to like *How to Run a Business*. I never had my mother's keen interest in all things business. It was just too spiritless for me.

Yet, the thought of opening an inn intrigued me. The thought came to me that I would have to do things like clean bathrooms, since who wants to share a bath with someone else's hair in the tub or toothpaste splatter on the mirror? And what about constantly making beds and changing linens, or finding someone's undies in the bottom of the sheets? Do you call the person and ask "Uhhh, what would you like me to do with your skivvies? Pitch 'em or mail 'em back?" Do I hire a cleaning lady?

Finally, the light went on in my head. I guess it would all be up to me. After all, I raised two boys all by myself, so, by God – I can do anything!

Months later, to my good fortune, I began dating a man who refinished antiques for a living and lent his expertise and services during auctions. It had been many years since I had dated and was really quite content. I loved my church and my house kept me busy. He was very creative and generous, and brought home treasures almost daily. Fabulous oil paintings, dressers, beds side tables, not to mention his creative furniture he made from antique pieces. I guess he came into my life at a time when I needed him. He didn't need me. I don't think he needed anybody. He was pretty happy just the way he was. You've heard of low maintenance? Well, he was NO maintenance. We started as great friends and many months later eventually became lovers. Our relationship eventually ended but he was a Godsend. I would have never had such a beautifully furnished home if it were not for him.

Armed with my B&B License in hand and the house freshly painted, I opened for business in the spring of 2006. The question now was, *how do I tell the rest of the world how to find Hull, Massachusetts - and me?* Typically, people who are looking to stay at a B&B will first search in cities they plan to visit. And though Boston is one of the top tourist cities in the world, Hull is not. After all the time I'd spent in Boston, I didn't even know Hull existed until my chance trip here with Jonathan. So how could I change that? I decided to do a little research and find out what other B&B owners do to attract customers. So, I typed 'Boston B&Bs' into my search engine and saw that there were listings for cities nearby to Hull. There's my answer, I thought!

I called the Bed and Breakfast website and asked about their advertising. I was thrilled to find it was low cost and affordable. Now, I needed to come up with a catchy name. Something that told people that my inn was special. Something that would compelled them to check out my website. I thought about terminology I could use to describe the Inn. I thought about what it was people were looking for in a B&B experience. I looked around my home and noticed how charming it was. I could say it was 'charming.' I looked out the window and saw how inviting the front porch was. I could say it was 'inviting.' Then, I looked across the street at the beach and the water and said, 'Oceanfront!' That's what people on vacation want in Massachusetts – oceanfront. I contacted the Bed and Breakfast website, told them what the name of my inn was The Coastal Cottage Inn. They even made the site for free (now, that was certainly affordable for me!) I just needed to forward photos. It worked well, and in no time at all I was up and running with bookings from people from all over the world!

Be My Guest

I often reflect on how sweet my guests were at the Coastal Cottage Inn. My very first guests never even stayed. The water heater gave out an hour before they arrived so I had to refer them to a nearby motel. They were very understanding but I was disappointed. But I wasn't going to let a little snafu like a broken water heater stop me. Gilligan fixed it the very next day and I was good to go.

Typical of the way things seemed to happen in my life, the people I needed tended to showed up when I needed them. And so is was with my first real guests, the ones who actually got to stay. They were from St. Austen, England. Of course, their accents were delightful and they made me feel encouraged because they had found my Inn from way across the 'pond,' as they say. They were innkeepers too, and were very considerate of me and my inexperience in the B&B world. They knew I had no clue what I was doing; I was quite upfront about that. Though I did not want to impose business on them during their vacation, they would give me all types of tips and tricks about the hospitality trade and seemed to enjoy helping. They, in essence, became my teachers for the short time they were with me. When they left, we exchanged numbers and promise to stay in touch. As first guests go, they were so charming and so very helpful. They gave me hope that I could really make this work. And for that, I will be forever grateful.

After that, the guests kept coming; just like the jobs that kept coming when I was struggling to make it as a model. I had the same thoughts and feelings about my new vocation as I did on the fashion runways in New York, *I can't believe I am getting paid to have this much fun!*

That first summer as an innkeeper was one of the most interesting, amusing, and unusual experiences of my life. I had received a phone call from a woman who was Ukrainian. She said she was having a fortieth birthday party for her husband Jeff Corwin, who was the lead in the series *Animal Planet*. For the party, they had invited friends from all over the country, if not the world, so she booked the entire house – all twenty rooms of it! They were going to arrive late in the evening so I left the front door unlocked (you could do that in Hull) so they could let themselves in. When I woke up the next morning and made my way downstairs to make breakfast, I was (remember, this was all new to me) quite surprised by what I found. In the living room, my beautifully furnished parlor, was a man sleeping on my cow skin rug on the floor - no pillow, no blanket - and the television blaring. I went to the linen closet and retrieved a pillow and blanket. As I propped his head on the pillow and draped the blanket over him, he just looked up at me, smiled, and went back to sleep. Another man was sprawled out on the couch, sound asleep. The smell of exhaled alcohol hung in the air. In the spare bedroom was yet another man who was so tall, half his body seemed to hang off of the little twin bed. It didn't look very comfortable to me but it didn't seem to bother him. He just lay there, like Gulliver in the land of Lilliputians, snoring away. When they woke, they were all pleasantly hung-over. They had been out all hours drinking at their friend's birthday party and had come back to the Inn to crash, and I mean *crash*! It was like I was running a frat house instead of an inn. But they were all very nice, not to mention (which I am going to anyway) good looking. And there wasn't any damage done, except for some of their brain cells.

It was really fun to get to know them and they loved my son's dog, Diablo, also known as D, a beautiful pit bull. Chris had finished his service in the Air Force and had returned to alive with me and Jonathan and brought his dog, just what I didn't need, a pit bull to entertain my guests. I gave the boys the in-law apartment to live in.

One man was a television producer, another a cameraman, and a couple were writers. When they left, I got big hugs all around. Shortly after, they sent pictures of D playing in my pond. They were certainly, an interesting group of guys.

At other times, I would rent the house to families who were having weddings in the area. Once, during the Head of the Charles Regatta rowing race, the German rowing team came to stay. They, too, were camped everywhere there was a flat soft surface. I knew there were more men than I had beds for so I purchased some air mattresses to put on the floor in the Great Room.

I discovered over time as an innkeeper that I was clearly not the only one with strong spiritual beliefs. When I would clean rooms, I would frequently find bibles that traveled with my guests. On one occasion, I awoke to some loud, strange, chanting. I went downstairs to find one of my Muslim guests doing prostrations on the floor praying to Allah. It made me smile and I went back to bed.

Year in and year out, I had a steady stream of guests from all walks of life. Periodically, I would get thank you cards from the travelers who stayed and I would often check out the comments posted after my guests left. I found that the Coastal Cottage Inn was gaining quite a nice reputation. The reviews posted to Bed and Breakfast on line were very positive so within no time at all, I was above a 4-star rating.

One morning I received a telephone call from the editor of *Golf Digest*. He said the magazine was considering running a story about B&Bs in the area and he had heard that my inn might be a good one to include in the article. Though I didn't read *Golf Digest* or even play the game, I thought that being featured in their magazine would be exciting, and free advertising. He went on to tell me that, while he and his wife searched the internet for my website, they found that the Coastal Cottage Inn website had been hacked. I wasn't very tech savvy so wasn't quite sure what he meant by hacked, though it sounded awful. He told me that when they found my site and clicked on the links for the rooms, they saw naked people doing...well...what naked people do. Apparently, that the links for my site had been redirected to, of all things, a porn site! Jokingly, he said it was obvious, from the wonderful reviews about my inn on the internet that the naked people from the porn site weren't fornicating in our bedrooms.

After my call with the editor concluded, I contacted the hosting site and told them to fix the link problem, immediately. It was pretty embarrassing to say the least. But all's well that ends well, and a month later, my home, my Coastal Cottage, my hard work was featured in a national magazine. And that was pretty cool.

Then there was Morty and Esther. They were hysterical and livened up my life and the lives of my guests. They were the cutest Jewish couple from New Jersey. They were in their late 60s and had been living together for years, unbeknownst to their children, which begged the question: Didn't their children ever come to visit?

They had booked the room at the end of the hall, so they needed to share a bathroom down with the other guests at the Inn, which is a pretty standard arrangement for a B&B. (None of my rooms, except the in-law apartment and mine, had their own bathrooms.) Early one morning, the whole house woke to the sound of Esther pounding on the bathroom door and shouting to Morty, who was in taking a shower. It went something like this:

POUND! POUND! POUND!

"MORTY! MORTY! OPEN THE DAHM DOHR and GEHT THE SHAMPOOOO!"

"I DON'T NEED IT!"

"MORTY! YA GOTTA WASH YAH HAIHR!"

"NO, I DID ALREADY!"

"YOU COULDINA. I GOT THE SHAMPOOO RIGHT HEAH! OPEN THE GAWHD DAHMND DOHR!"

Shortly afterward, you could hear the shower turn off and the door open. From the bathroom you could hear Esther giving Morty holy hell for trying to get away with not washing his hair; probably just like his mother used to do. Like I said, they were cute.

Another of my guests was a former Swiss Consul and his beautiful wife. She had worked with Nelson Mandela and the African National Congress on the signing of the Geneva Conventions in the

1980s. She was also a concert pianist and had come to Boston to attend a seminar at the Berkley School of Music. Interestingly, the seminar was about the healing effects of music on people, which was certainly a concept I could believe in. During their visit she would sit at the piano in the living room and play the most beautiful melodies.

One evening, I lit some candles and while her husband and I sat on the sofa, she played the piano. As the notes filled the air, the flame from the candles and the waves framed by the windows behind her, moved in concert with the melody. It was so peaceful and relaxing, I felt almost hypnotized. I was in awe of how she could affect my mind, body and spirit by just the touch of her fingers on the ivories.

To my further amazement, she told me afterward that the music she played was not a predefined composition, not something she had learned from a sheet of music. The music, she said, came to her at the piano and was different every time and something she had never played before. When I asked her how she did it, she said she just sat at the piano, focused on the moment, and picked up the vibrations in the room.

To my great pleasure, she had recorded her performance for me that night. Even today when I listen to it, it brings me back to that night in my living room. I feel so relaxed and renewed. I feel healed.

And sometimes, the guests who came to the Coastal Cottage Inn were there, I believe, because they were where they needed to be at a time they needed to be there - and not for the charm of an old New England B&B, the ocean or the Hull beaches - but something else. When people pack for vacation, they not only bring their clothes, their toothbrushes, and shaving kits, they also bring their heartaches, their sorrows, and their pain. Such was a couple that came to stay at my inn.

I was busy preparing the Inn for guests, which is what I was always doing, with love of course, when the doorbell rang. I answered it and saw a woman standing on the porch. She said her husband and she had reservations to stay and wanted to know where they should park. Her husband, who was in the car on the street, shouted up to her on the deck. He sounded quite angry and frustrated. I could see that it made the woman nervous so I went down to the car to try and calm him and to show him where to park. He looked a bit embarrassed being caught cussing.

After he'd parked the car and came in, I gave them their key and room number and led them upstairs. They stayed in their room for hours before coming down to take a walk on the beach.

When they returned from their walk, he went up to the room and she joined me on the deck, taking the seat next to mine facing the ocean. It was getting to be dusk and the moon was rising, seemingly, from the ocean depths. I sat quietly reading. She just stared out at the water. Then all of a sudden, she started crying uncontrollably. I put the book down and went to her. I wrapped my arms around her and asked if there was anything I could do.

"I can't believe I am doing this. I am so sorry," she said through her sobs. I told her it was all right, not to worry about it, to do what she needed to do. She tried to compose herself but it was of no use, the tears just kept coming.

After a while, she gained control of her emotions and was able to speak. She shared with me that her son had committed suicide, leaving behind a wife and two young children. He had lost his job, she continued, and was deep in debt. And though it was hard on everyone, her husband couldn't get over it. She said it was the first time he had left the house in a year. It was her idea to come to Hull where his friends were playing in a band at the Sea Note Bar. He didn't want to come but she pried him loose from the house to come and thought it would be good for him, and for them. But, now, she wasn't so sure it was a very good idea. He was as unhappy here as he was there; he was inconsolable. She cried some more. I listened patiently and let her cry. When I thought she was ready to hear it, I told her that God works in mysterious ways. And though it might sound like a pat answer for people in pain, I knew it to be true.

"You," I continued, "have been brought here by God." I told her that my first husband had killed himself, leaving me with a two-year old child to raise on my own. I knew the guilt, the doubt, the anguish, and the void people feel when a loved one commits suicide. The act itself is an indictment and a life sentence.

"But I am here today to tell you," I reassured her, "that they - your daughter-in-law and your grandchildren - will be okay! And you and your husband will heal."

She listened and continued to cry. She said it was the first time since learning of her son's death that she had cried. And now, the tears would not stop. I held her as she cried over the loss of her son for the first time. When she had no more tears to shed, she went back to her room and to her husband. Later that evening, when they returned from the "Sea Note" where they watched his friends' band play, her husband came out to the porch and thanked me. He gave me a big hug. The frustration in his eyes from when I first saw him was gone, he was now at peace. It made me smile inwardly, because, as I said, I believe people show up where they need to be, when they need to be there. I helped them to release some of their pent-up grief. And I believe, someday, they will be somewhere when someone needs them to share their story. And I believe when that times comes, they will be happy to do it, like I was.

Once a lady called to book a room for her sister. She said she wanted to come and take a look at the Inn because her sister was from the Hamptons in New York and a bit of a prima donna. She would be staying for a week and wanted to make sure there wouldn't be anything for her sister to bitch about. Wow, I couldn't wait to have her as my guest!!!

While sitting on the front porch with some of my quests we watched as a lady walked up the front walkway. The walkway was in disrepair as I was having slate stones installed and with the construction project going on, she had to walk around the chaos on the walk. I asked her if I could assist her. She told me she was the one who called to see if the place was suitable for her sister. She turned to leave and said, "I don't think she's going to like it here."

I knew she was judging the place form the exterior. Being the kind of person, I am, I assured her she would be comfortable and insisted she come inside to look around. She found it very lovely and booked the room, as I knew she would.

When her sister arrived, she was in a rental car and asked for help getting some of her things out of the car. As I looked at the number of suitcases crammed in the truck, I couldn't believe she was *only staying a week*. She said her 'driver' usually handled 'these things.'

I jokingly added, "Well, if you want, I'll drive you around. Let me see if I have a tux in the attic."

She just looked at me but I saw a hint of a smile across her face.

After she settled in she loved her room and spent a lot of time on the deck smoking cigarettes and staring out at the ocean. Days went by and she had yet to visit her sister, so I asked if she was feeling well. She said she didn't care much for her sister and found it quite pleasant exactly right where she was, doing what she was doing. We began talking and before I knew it, it all came pouring out. She said she was going to get a divorce after 30 years of marriage. Her husband was in his 70s, overweight, very wealthy, very well connected, and a cheat! He had apparently, done the typical man thing and left her for a young girl old enough to be his granddaughter.

When she told me about how the girl made him wear jeans five sizes too big, which made his butt hang out as if he were one of her adolescent boyfriends, she laughed so hard at the mental picture that she had tears running down her face. She said that the best part of the ridiculousness of his affair, particularly since he didn't seem aware that his friends at the county club were all making fun of him. She hadn't seen it for herself she said, but could not stop laughing at the image it conjured.

She was an attractive woman with Elizabeth Taylor eyes that were the deepest lavender blue I've ever seen. Poor Gilligan (my handyman) wouldn't leave her alone. He kept trying to get her to go have a drink with him. Jokingly, I told her she could go back home and tell her friends she had an affair with a younger man. "Don't wealthy women have fantasies about the Portuguese pool boys?" I asked. She just chuckled.

We became pretty close after awhile and I could tell she was starting to feel better as the days passed. She enjoyed the inn and the camaraderie it offered as she extended her trip an extra week. Sally and I would sit with her in the evenings, cocktails in hand, and discuss the male species at length (no pun intended -- well, maybe a little bit).

She decided she would move out of the home when she returned to the Hamptons. We talked about the things she would take and the things she would leave behind. When it came to the silverware, silver service and tea set and other assorted silver items, we put our heads together to figure out who she was going to give it all to. She was determined the damn new woman -- young girl really -- wasn't going to end up with it!

We finally decided that it go to her maid in Bermuda, after all, she said she always liked her.

When she checked-out she gave me a beautiful pink blouse as a gift and a beautiful, big, warm hug as a 'thank you.' We said our good-byes and I wished her well.

Another day I returned from my early morning walk to the ocean to find one of my guests sitting at the kitchen table having his coffee. I sat down and joined him and asked what he did for a living. He told me that he was a space engineer and was part of the team that launched the Mars Rover. We talked about how it went through the different atmospheric layers to get to Mars. It was as if I had a live NOVA series playing out at my kitchen table.

A couple came to the Inn because the husband was going to see a specialist in Boston. He had been diagnosed with mesothelioma and was afraid he was going to die. I did something that I rarely do. I went up into my little house chapel, gathered my holy oil from my collection of articles from the Holy land and I put some on his forehead. A month later when they returned for their follow up visit, he told me *the disease was gone*. He was convinced it was my oil. Who knows? I'm just glad it had a good ending.

Another family that came to stay as guests were Mormons. They had won a trip from one the airlines and chose to stay at my place. They were rather poor and spent most the time near the house on the beach. I shared with them my childhood experiences with the Mormon faith. They seemed concerned about my perspective on their religion. After they checked out, I found *The Book of Mormon* in the little boy's room with a note on top. It said he wanted me to have the book. The note went onto say that it was his and it had given him a lot of strength. It wasn't *The Book of Mormon* that I loved. It was the generosity of the heart of the little boy that was so endearing.

Then there was a couple who visited from the Mid-West. The wife had been going through chemotherapy and her husband promised that once she felt better he would take her to the ocean, which she had never seen before. While at the inn, she would join Sally and me on the deck where we all laughed hysterically. She was such a vibrant soul that we let her join our 'little girls club.' Five days later, after they checked out, I found a very sweet letter from her husband and a hundred-dollar tip. He said that he hadn't heard her laugh that hard in months. And I was glad, for my little part, that we, Sally and me, could bring a little laughter back into her life. I took the hundred dollars and planted perennials in the front yard to remind me of her and all the poor souls battling cancer.

Between the drunk partiers and the piano-playing healers and the people who needed healing, I was enjoying my new vocation. And, truthfully, couldn't imagine doing anything else. I'd met a lot of different people in my life and had had good and bad experiences with them all, from politicians to garbage truck drivers. I guess Hebrews 13:2 was right. I guess I had entertained many angels unawares, in the five short years I ran my inn.

If There's a Will, There's a Way

During the winters, when bookings for the Inn were nil, I would close the Inn and go to Utah to work at the ski resorts. I hated to leave the house abandoned, though I knew George and Sally would keep an eye on it. But it seemed like an imposition considering that they had their restaurant to manage. And I was always just a little nervous about it being empty for months at a time. So, one year, I decided to get someone to help with the guests and house-sit when I was away. I figured that they could look after the Inn and be available for the guests in the spring, before I returned from Utah. I thought it was a swell plan.

I used to see her walking across the road to the beach with her four-year-old daughter, whom she was raising by herself. She would sometimes visit her mother who lived in the section 8 housing next door to me. Knowing full well what it was like to be the sole support for a toddler, I thought I'd be doing us both a favor if I rented one of my suites to her for the low price of four hundred dollars a month, in exchange for her help with the guests. I wouldn't even require a security deposit. When I made my proposal, she accepted right away and was very excited about the opportunity. Shortly after accepting, she moved her things to the Inn. I closed off part of the Inn that had its own entrance and made her a studio apartment, that's when the real fun started.

Now that she was all settled in, she came and went whenever she wanted, which was her prerogative -- I wasn't her mother. It got pretty old though, when every time I needed her help with the guests on the weekends, she was never around. She would be off in New

York, Boston, or Botswana for all I knew. And though she didn't pay a security deposit, she didn't pay any of the agreed upon $400.00 rent either. After a couple of months of this nonsense, I confronted her and telling her that the arrangement was not working out. She told me that she was looking for work, which I didn't believe. Someone at the George and Sally's Corner Café had already informed me that she had done this before and would use the little girl as her meal ticket. I mean, who would want to throw a little girl out on the street. It was a despicable type of ruse because, no matter the circumstances, you could never quite feel good about the results. But as I soon figured out that she was nothing more than a scam artist, taking advantage of people whenever she could, I decided she had to go. I felt bad about the decision particularly because there was a child involved. But things could not go on the way they were. I did not, however, understand how hard it was going to be to rid my house of this parasite.

Every time I asked her to find another place to live she had an excuse, and all of them feeble! I too, had been a single mom and I never had those excuses. Her father seemed like a good guy but she said his new wife didn't want her around. Though I had compassion for her situation, I could not adopt a full-grown woman with a daughter. I had to exorcise her from my life. And since she wouldn't leave, I went to the courthouse to have her evicted. I filled out all the paperwork and waited my turn for the clerk to help me with the process. Then, to my utter dismay, I was informed that once I served her with an eviction notice, she had 30 days to vacate. But if she still wouldn't leave, she had another 30 days before she'd have to go to court. And then, after the case was heard, the judge could allow her another six months to or even longer because she had a child to consider.

I was flabbergasted, flummoxed, and frustrated! I couldn't believe that this person could be in my home for the next eight months, coming and going as she pleased, irritating me and my son, and all rent free! I had heard that no good deed goes unpunished but I always thought that that was a rather cynical view of the world.

Even more deplorable than squatting in my home was that she was using her little girl to live rent free, knowing the courts would not make her move until she had somewhere else to go. She even gave her boyfriend, who had just gotten out of jail for drug trafficking and his friends' keys to my home! Clearly, *she needed to go.*

I had Gilligan come over and shut off the hot water to the bathroom so she couldn't take a hot shower. But after a couple days she threatened to sue me. I contacted the courts, yet again, only to find out that I could get into serious trouble for denying her the luxury of hot water, though she denied me the basic obligation of rent.

For the next month, I sat by and watched her and her boyfriend come and go as if they owned the place. I felt like I was being bound and gagged while others, including the officers of the town of Hull, watched and did nothing. The police said it was a Civil Case. It drove me absolutely crazy! And, as if being scammed by this little hustler wasn't bad enough, I was losing income because I could not rent the suite to my B&B guests and was spending money on court fees and eviction notices. I had gotten so desperate; I even offered her two thousand dollars if she would just leave. She refused and instead sought the advice of her uncle, an attorney, who advised her to demand I pay her first, and last month's rent, security deposit, and all moving expenses for a new apartment of her choice, which could have easily totaled nine thousand dollars or more! I could not believe that any human being would do that to another. And I could not believe that my home was, in essence, being held for ransom. And I couldn't believe that there was nothing I could do about it. Well, almost nothing.

Sally and I, as usual, were sitting on my deck, having an after-work cocktail and trying to figure out how we were going to get her out of my house. We had already tried playing loud Polka music outside her door at 6:30 in the morning but to no avail; she took it in stride. I guess there is a lot one will put up with for a free ride. Finally, after mulling over all sorts of schemes, I devised a plan, and, if it didn't work, nothing would.

The plan was to get some raw fish and while she was away on one of her many New York weekend trips with her boyfriend, we would hide raw fish in the apartment. After a day or two, when the fish started to rot, the smell would force her to leave. We laughed at the appropriateness of the plan; you know what they say about fish and guests after three days, and agreed that it needed to be done! It was the only thing left to do!

Sally ran down to the restaurant and brought me back a few cans of sardines in olive oil (for those who are cholesterol conscious). I also ran across the street to the fresh fish market and got a sea bass and chopped it into small pieces, then grabbed the ladder and we furtively went up the staircase to her suite. When we got her door, we conspiringly looked down the hall to the right, then the left. Why? I have no idea. We were the only ones at home. Once inside, I got up on the ladder and placed the oily, marinated fish inside the antique stained-glass chandelier. The darkened glass hid the muck so she wouldn't see it. Then we folded up the ladder, took one last look at our handiwork and left, giggling the whole time.

A few hours later, Sally came back to the Inn with a special present from her cat, Rascal. She said that Rascal wanted to help us out and handed me a small paper bag. I took the bag and opened it, not sure of what I would find. It was from a cat so it could have been several different things. I peeked in the bag and saw a freshly-killed mouse! I looked at Sally and we burst out laughing like a couple of naughty children. Back up to the room we went. I took out the mouse and pushed it way up into the antique radiator. Then we retreated from our secret mission and waited.

I had expected that it would only take a few days for the raw fish, sardines and the mouse to let their presence be known but I heard and smelled nothing. A few more days, and nothing! I was beginning to worry that not only would the plan fail, I would be stuck with her non-paying presence in my home until her daughter went off to college. A couple weeks went by with nothing. She must have thought I had horrible allergies always sniffing as I passed by her door, waiting for any sign of decay.

Then, July 4th – Independence Day came. The intruder and her boyfriend went away for the holiday weekend. Temperatures soared to above one hundred degrees and it seemed as though nature herself was in cahoots with Sally and me. The long-awaited decay started. The suite began to smell so bad I stuffed old towels under the door so the smell would not get into the rest of the Inn. The only thing left to do was to sit back and watch what would happen. Hopefully, the smell wouldn't get into the rest of the house.

She and her boyfriend finally returned from their weekend trip around 2:00 am in the morning. I watched her from my bedroom window where I could see from the top floor, down into the parking lot. They went in and out of the apartment all night long.

The next day, I went and banged on the door to her apartment. When she opened it, the smell that emanated from inside was rank and putrid. How she could even spend one night in that stench was beyond me. She had only been home for a few hours. I complained that there was a horrible odor coming from her apartment and she needed to do something about it. Her face had the look of someone who had just taken a bite of a bitter lemon, she was clearly disgusted by the odor herself. She said she had no idea what was causing it, that she and her boyfriend spent the entire night looking for it. When she said that, I think but cannot be sure, that my eyes involuntarily looked up at the chandelier. In the game of poker, it would have been a 'tell' I suppose, but she didn't seem to notice.

Within two hours, she was all packed, her father loaded all her stuff into his truck and, thank God, she was gone. I had my home back.

As soon as she disappeared down the street, I put on my rubber gloves and a painter's mask, not that it could filter out the rot that filled the air, but it was still better than nothing. In the apartment, I climbed the ladder to the chandelier and removed the fish that had become an oozing, slimy paste. I located the now maggot-filled mouse, pulled it from its resting place and threw it a plastic bag and tied it once, twice, even three times. The grossness of the job was nothing compared to the hell that girl had put me through. Then I sprayed bleach on every surface in the room, cleaned all the windows, and opened every door and window in the house. It took about three hours for the smell to dissipate. As a parting gift, her boyfriend put a bunch of towels and blankets in the shower and turned on the water to flood the bathroom.

I will never forget the important lessons I learned from that experience. One is that not all sweet, innocent girls are sweet and innocent; and another is, if you open the dictionary and look up the definition of *a true friend*, you will find a photo of my pal Sally!

The rest of the summer went very well and in the fall l headed to Utah to make plans for the winter there.

My Coastal Cottage Inn in Hull, Massachusetts

Me (L), Jonathan (C), and Sally (R) during one of our days of silliness

Chapter 10: Kismet

Beauty is not in the face; beauty is a light in the heart. – Kahlil Gibran

Two Strangers at an Airport

I secured a part time job at one of the ski resorts for the winter of 2009 and did not want to return to Boston. I felt glad to be back with my family. I was very fond of my little niece, Tiara, and enjoyed going to my sister's barber shop, The Gambler, to get my hair done. I felt at home in both Boston and Utah.

The previous summer was the summer of my discontent with the home invasion of the unwanted girl. I decided to break up with Jay, my live-in boyfriend - it just wasn't working. I guess I couldn't blame him. I was always away in the winters with family and he stayed in Boston without me. Jay had many wonderful traits and in the end, we still remain dear friends.

I had a flight scheduled on Friday, September 5th, to go back to Boston to close up the Inn for the season. But on Thursday night, when I went to bed, I had the most awful, apprehensive feeling. Though it took me a while, I finally fell asleep, but only to wake at 2:00 in the morning with horrible chest pains. Not the *rush-to-the-hospital-in-case-it's-a-heart-attack* pain but from a strong intuition NOT to board that plane. It was not the first time I had a premonition and I wasn't about to ignore my feeling, so it was settled. I was not going on that particular flight. I called the cab company and cancelled my morning taxi ride to the airport. I didn't care. I wasn't leaving. With that resolved, the panic in my chest eased and I fell asleep.

The next morning, I slept in and awoke feeling great. I called Jay and told him I would not be on the flight.

"Are you kidding?" Jay responded. "You've got B&B guests.

The terrible guilt for not being at the Inn to say good-bye to my last guests for the season set in, so I found myself dashing to the airport trying to book a later flight. The only flights available however, were for the next day. Though I didn't realize it at the time, luck was smiling down on me. My flight back to Boston now departed from Salt Lake City with a layover in Phoenix and a layover in Las

Vegas, then on to Boston, arriving at Logan at 1:00 in the morning. I called Jay and asked him to play Innkeeper until I could get home.

Sitting at the Phoenix airport, while drinking my second glass of wine and eating a bad hamburger, I noticed a handsome man walking in the terminal across from me. As I watched him, I thought about how I had such bad luck choosing my partners. I knew what I wanted in a man but still ended up with the wrong ones. The thoughts, having had their say, left me alone. I sat unmindful, going into my own mental world. I didn't even see him approach until he looked down at me and said, "How come you look so pensive?"

I thought to myself, *'What business is it of yours?'*

"Where you going?" he said.

I was mildly surprised to see that it was the same man I had noticed earlier in the terminal. I looked at him more closely. He was tall and ruggedly handsome with big beautiful blue captivating eyes. I found his salt and pepper hair and happy demeanor quite appealing and sexy. He looked quite comfortable and confident in blue jeans, a striped shirt, and blue blazer. His shoes gave him away, though. A clean Italian loafer means they are ego driven and want to flaunt their status. Worn tennis shoes show they really don't care about much except sports and are pretty easy going. Worn boat shoes usually mean they are successful and adventurous. He was wearing worn-out boat shoes (love them) and looked just like Mark Harmon from NCIS. I told him I was headed to Boston. He said he was going to L.A. to visit his brother and family.

"Where are you from?" I asked.

"Washington, DC."

Oh, a politician, I thought.

"You look like you're from Annapolis!" I responded.

Now, to this day, I do not know why those words shot out of my mouth. They just came to mind and then fell off my lips. I knew nothing about Annapolis. I had never been there or even thought about going there. He looked shocked at my comment and extended his hand to show me his ring, which was gold with a big blue stone. It was his college graduation ring from the United States Naval Academy in Annapolis. He sat down without being asked, ordered a beer for himself and another glass of wine for me. We had an instant attraction. We just fit! As we talked over the next two hours, our eyes never left each other. We talked about our current situation with our partners. Neither of us was happy in our relationships and were planning to end them soon. He told me his sister was a Buddhist nun and that he had had three failed marriages. So, he had one-upped me there, I thought. He said he had a handsome, funny brother, two incredibly talented sisters, and a seventeen-year-old daughter. He came to tears when he told me that they hadn't spoken since he deployed to Iraq. He was a retired Navy Captain, worked as a defense analyst, did sculpture, wrote a musical and a screenplay, and did some part-time acting in theater.

When it was time for me to catch my flight, he walked me to my plane and shook my hand. I could still smell his cologne after I boarded my flight. It made me smile. I was certainly on a strange high after meeting him. The farther I flew away from him the more I began to realize that my life had just changed course.

On my flight from Phoenix to Vegas I sat next to a cute little six-year-old girl who was traveling alone to go see her father. When I learned she was traveling by herself, I told the flight attended I would watch over her. She was very content to be sitting on a plane full of strangers and coloring. While filling in a picture of a rose in her coloring book, she looked up at me and asked if I was married. I replied no, I wasn't.

With all the wisdom of a child, she asked me, "Do you know who you're supposed to marry?"

I replied that I didn't.

"If you ever found your head on someone's shoulder while they stroked my hair, then that's who you're supposed to marry."

I thought what an interesting comment coming from such a little girl but figured that she was just excited about seeing her father.

On my next flight from Las Vegas to Boston, I sat with a couple from Connecticut. They had been together for many years but weren't married. Over the next six hours, I found myself telling them all about my life. I even told them about the man I had just met at the Phoenix airport. They both listened intently.

After several hours of me chatting mostly with the woman, the man who had sat just listening the whole time looked over at me and said, "I think you're going to end up with the guy you just met in the airport."

I don't know if it was something in my eyes that gave away my feelings for the stranger at the Phoenix airport or just a feeling that the man on the plane had, but it was odd to think that a chance meeting could become something more than that – two people killing time, waiting for a flight.

The Virtual Date

Marcus called me a few days after I arrived home. "What are you doing?" he asked.

"I'm futzing around the kitchen." I replied.

"Good," he said, "I'm there with you."

With his words in my ear, I looked out the window that faced the Atlantic Ocean and imagined him there with me. "How about we take a glass of wine and walk across the street to the beach?" I said.

"Let's take the bottle," he replied.

He then began to describe our virtual date.

"We're putting our blanket on the sand and laughing. We're sitting down and drinking our wine and laughing some more, listening to the waves dissipating on the shore. I'm leaning over and running my fingers through your hair and then I ask if I can kiss you. But, because it's our first kiss it must be careful, cautious, long and slow. Many more will follow and then we will laugh again. I put my arms over your shoulders and pull you back and kiss you again."

My head was swimming with just a little bit of imaginary wine and his romantic vision.

"What now?" I asked him.

"We're walking back to your house. We are at the front door."

I interjected, "We have to go wash the sand off our feet first. It's hard on the hardwood floors."

"Oh, yeah," he replied.

Quickly he went back to our fantastical date. "We're now standing at your front door. I kiss you again, scoop you up into my arms and carry you into the house. Having never been in your home I don't know what room to take you to though."

"Well," I asked, "how long have we known each other?"

"Several months," he replied.

"My bedroom then," I said.

We finished the virtual date by making love, and with him holding me all night. In the morning we make love again, as we watch the sun rise over the Atlantic.

A few days later my friend Franny came from Montana for a visit. We – Franny, Jay, and me - went to an antique show in Brimfield, Massachusetts. While Jay meandered off looking at antiques in the show, I told Franny about meeting Marcus and our virtual date. She told me that I should forget about him, that he was probably married. And, not only that, long distance relationships didn't work. I stood there listening to her advice and holding a large hourglass I was admiring when my cell phone rang. It was Marcus.

When I answered it, he said, "We are like sands in the hourglass."

I about fainted! "Oh my God," I said, "I'll call you right back. I want to send you a photo of what is in my hand!"

I was just so astounded. I told Franny what he had said. She merely replied, "Beee caaaareful."

I knew she was looking out for me in her way but I felt that there was something going on here that was just too coincidental to be, well, a coincident. I told her about all the events and happenings that led up to our meeting and beyond. I told her about cancelling my flight, his first appearance in passing, the fact that I knew he was from Annapolis without him saying so, that his sister was a nun, the fact that I was holding an hourglass while he called, and a few other strange connections. I called them 'kismets.' She called them nonsense.

Jay had purchased an original oil painting by Hester Adlercron of a mountain snow scene at the antique show. He was curious about the artist and its origins so Franny said she would do some research on it when she returned to Montana. Before she left, she made me promise to forget about Marcus. She didn't want me to get hurt. I didn't want to get hurt anymore either and agreed that I would. But I so loved the sound of his baritone voice. I could not get it, or him, out of my mind. It was a pleasant refrain that played in my mind often. He had sent me emails with photos of himself and I sent him some of me. Our communication stopped, however, when I asked if he had broken off his relationship with his girlfriend yet. I received no answer, which I considered my answer. I became convinced Fran was right. He was probably married.

A few weeks after my last email to Marcus, I sat admiring the Adlercron painting that hung on my living room wall when the phone rang. It was Franny.

"I've finished the research on the painting" she said. "It was painted in the early 1900s. Hester's grandfather was George Bancroft, former Secretary of the Navy and the founder of Naval Academy in Annapolis. She married a British captain and moved to London. Her mother was a famous sculptor."

My head started reeling. My heart started connecting the dots. Marcus sculpted as a hobby, was a Navy Captain, went to the Naval Academy, and had lived in Bancroft Hall. That was IT! Some clues we get in life just cannot be ignored. I had to find out what was going on. There were too many 'kismets.' I had to go to Annapolis. I called him as soon as I hung up with her. He, too, agreed that there was something strange going on. I booked a flight to Maryland and he agreed to pick me up. I asked him to get me a room at one of the B&B's in the area.

Marcus met me at the curb after I landed at Baltimore Washington International. When I got in his car, he leaned over and kissed me. It wasn't like our first virtual kiss on the beach but we had an air of excitement around us. We vibrated happy together. There was definitely something magical happening.

The day was perfect. It was 72 degrees and clear, blue skies. We drove to the Annapolis historical district where we checked into our room. The Annapolis Boat Show was going on that weekend and we were lucky to get a room. Thank God, there were two beds, as I had requested. He kissed me again. I loved the shape of his mouth and how well it fit on mine. We were so good together. He never once let go of my hand. He took me over to Bancroft Hall and as we walked through the exhibits, he showed me all the heroes of the Navy who had once lived there. I was so enchanted by his attention, I couldn't concentrate on what he was saying. I knew nothing about Maritime History and I couldn't get over how good I felt being with him.

Between the weather and Marcus, it was a glorious day for a boat show. We stopped to sit on a bench facing the marina. An old couple walked by, stopped and smiled. They told us that we made a very cute couple. We agreed with that and went into McGarvey's, an Irish pub, where we shared calamari, beer, wine, great kisses and conversation.

As we walked around the town he did voice imitations and sang me short song riffs from musicals. We laughed and kissed and kissed some more. We went back to our room to get ready for dinner and the energy between us was electrifying. I wore my new crushed velvet gold summer dress and he wore his blazer, a maroon sweater, and nice gray pants. Everywhere we went people would complement us on what a great couple we made, how beautiful we looked together.

We had dinner at the Treaty of Paris Inn, a place where George Washington, Ben Franklin, and the whole founding father gang used to hang out. While I was looking up at the waiter, giving him my order, I felt a very warm glow inside my chest. It was so intense I turned and looked directly at Marcus. He was staring right into my eyes, with his beautiful, beautiful eyes!

"You know what I just said to you?" He asked. He had told me, without saying a word, that he was falling in love with me but I felt it.

I smiled at him to let him know that I had felt it and he said, "Yes. Yes, Pamela. I am."

After dinner we strolled towards the marina. He took my hands and started to dance with me along the sidewalk. Turning me round and round, singing the melody of 'Singing in the Rain,' although it was not raining! It was so much fun. A young couple stopped us, complimented me on my dress, Marcus on his great dancing, and asked us for a light for their cigarette. Then the girl told me to make a wish because my cross I wore on my neck was flipped around. She then told Marcus how beautiful I was.

"Are you looking at her?" she said to him with a drunken slur.

"Yes." he said. "I've been looking at her all night."

"Don't screw this up with her" she told him, as if a warning. "She is amazing."

The girl was drunk, but there are no coincidences. Even I felt it was a warning from beyond!

We went back to the hotel room and I got into bed with my pajamas on. Marcus climbed in next to me. We both agreed that if we were to die that next day, we would have died perfectly happy. He held me and kissed me but not in the manner of foreplay. It was just tender and loving. I knew he was still living with the girlfriend and, in that instant, I was glad. Though it had been a perfect day, I could not have made love to him. It was too soon and I wanted our first time to be right and true – just like our feelings for each other. And he, of course, was not only an officer but a perfect gentleman.

When I woke the next morning, just as the little girl had said, my head was on his shoulder, his fingers gently stroking my hair! I then felt an undeniable state of being, I was falling in love. Or perhaps, I was already there.

After we rose and checked out of the B&B, we gabbed a cup coffee and he drove me to the airport. As I walked along with the other travelers to catch my flight, he called to me. I turned around and he said, "I love you."

Chapter 11: The Moneychangers

Then Jesus entered the temple of God and drove out all who sold and bought in the temple, and he overturned the tables of the money changers and the seats of those who sold pigeons. He said unto them, "It is written, 'My house shall be called a house of prayer'; but you make it a den of robbers." – Matthew 21: 12-13

Heavenward

The Bag Lady shooed away a larger bird from her little group of sparrows trying to take away their food. Her movement broke my memories and brought me back to the present. It seemed as though half a lifetime had passed and she had been patiently listening to me all the while. The old woman then spoke to me gently and with great wisdom.

"Our success," she said, "comes entirely from the hand of the Lord. Human pride, however, says that we are the ones! WE have the POWER! So, we build our towers of Babel. We want the universe at our disposal. We dream of thrones beyond the clouds, but no one and nothing really submits to us. The powerless of man is demonstrated over and over by his falls, yet he continues to seek his own will be done rather than giving into the will of God. Nothing and no one can harm a man. He only harms himself because of his wrong choices."

"Isn't it ironic that Judas fell while in the presence of the Savior yet the righteous were saved in Sodom?" the old woman asked as she tilted her head closer to mine.

"You see? Look how we never learn. We go to war over and over again. We never just stop to trust in the Creator," she then looked up skyward with her eyes.

"We feed ourselves with pleasure and beautiful things," she continued. "We strive for luxury at any cost. Then we kill and hate and do horrible things to keep what we think we deserve. The more a man has, the more he tries to hold onto it, the more damage he does in doing so; hence the current state of affairs."

"Pretty lady," her voice crackled, "I am sorry for your losses and the way some have treated you. I am sorry people have tried to destroy *your heart. The Lord is love. Even when the Lord failed and railed against the moneychangers in the Temple, He still showed us the right way."*

After a moment of reflection, she spoke again, "You know, there are many men, perpetually lost in the dark, who have thought that money, prestige, and power rule the day. In a way, they are right, if you want to stay on a lower level of consciousness. But that will never bring peace."

She then commented on the insane traffic in gold, the drive-thru, instant fortunes to be made on Wall Street, and how they are as ruinous to the country as they are to the parties engaged in them.

"Few fail who are honest, earnest, and patient," she said, "and true success involves avoiding all speculations such as the stock market." She had seen the frenzy that comes over the brokers' board on Wall Street, with its babble of conflicting sounds and, what she referred to as a 'hot oven' that few can withstand for lone. She thought it as dangerous as the lottery.

I had another question to ask; Why did she keep living this way, on the street where people either abused or ignored her.

She said, "As I got older, my senses and intuitions became stronger, so much so that when I'm around other people, I can feel their emotional energy."

Most people, she explained, had a lot of 'ick' they carried with them through life. And if she engaged with them, they would suck the positive life particles out of her, so she found it more peaceful to be alone. She chose to wander and, sometimes, when the time arose, she'd meet people who needed her insights or needed to be warned about something impending in their lives. She seemed to consider herself a guardian angel of sorts.

"I guess we have quite a bit in common," I told the woman. I often picked up on negative energy emanating from people as well, and it made me feel unwanted, unloved because they felt unwanted or unloved. I truly believe that we become the energies we associate ourselves with, or rather the people we associate with, the music we listen to, the movies we watch, and the books we read. It and we are all connected.

"I found an amazing faith in God," she continued, "I saw God. Only those with a pure heart can see God."

Now I understood the source of the old woman's glow; it was her faith in God.

For me, I had lived between heaven and hell, all due to my choices. I thought about the men I chose to love and marry and remembered my mother cautioning me, saying that the most important decision I would ever make in life is who I chose for a husband.

"That choice," she said, "will make you or break you." And I often wonder what decisions I would have made if I had taken her words seriously. Instead, along came a stream of men who nearly broke me.

"After my husband died," I continued to tell the Bag Lady, "I enrolled at the University of Utah. I wanted to go to college to broaden myself. I truly wanted to be a doctor. But one day, while I was studying for a psychology test, my father said, 'What the hell are you even going to college for? You're so screwed up, you need a psychiatrist!'"

"I forgave my father," I continued, "when I found out he had his baby died in his arms. I learned when I was a child not to judge, just like it says in the Bible – 'Judge not, lest you be judged.' I knew, and know, that a person is not in a state of love when they judge others and that a lot of peace comes from not passing judgment. An exercise I practice is to spend an entire day without having an opinion about anything. It is liberating."

The Bag Lady agreed, we did have much in common.

She continued, "Who truly knows the past of the mother who has just slapped her child in the store? Maybe she has to go home to an abusive husband and can no longer listen to the screaming. Or a former policeman who killed someone in the line of duty, someone who resembled his brother? Or the man at the stop light begging for cash might be a man who once carried his dying comrade from a battlefield in a senseless war. Maybe the one dollar you give to him will go to his alcohol, but if it kills his pain, then why not? Don't we all kill our own pain in one way or another? Some people kill their pains in life by being workaholics, cheating on their spouses or on their taxes, stealing, driving way too fast, buying things we can't afford, sexual addictions, or doing other things just to numb the pain. We don't know if the drunk passed out on the bench didn't bury his child years earlier. What about the mother in jail who is losing her son to a bad motorcycle accident – he is on life support and she is waiting to get a court order so she can sign papers to pull the plug on his lifeless body? Can we judge her actions after that? How do we know if the attractive *young girl selling her body to an escort service, or pole dancing at night isn't just trying to buy medicine or medical insurance for her children? The answer to all these questions and situations is that we can't know so we should not judge. Who knows, we may wind up in the same place someday and maybe not even because of our choices. Maybe it is because of the choices of someone else close to us who affected us deeply."*

I heard my new friend say that there are people in the world who, even though they are not given to prayer, see light, even in the darkest of rooms. It seems to emanate from every article in the room so much so that they can see things by it. And about people who see their doubles and can enter into the thoughts of other people.

As she passed her understanding to me, her heart was so full of sweetness and delight that no tongue can tell of it. Nor can it be likened to anything material. The grace of God came to her and that grace is beyond compare. Every other feeling is base compared to the sweet knowledge of grace found in the heart. Its power is so great that nothing, no degree of suffering can stand against it.

Bank Lending

I walked to the water ferry from the 'T'. I was so inspired by my new teacher, my new friend, and my encounter with the old Bag Lady that I felt a shift in consciousness. As I boarded and sat down on the ferry and gazed out the window at the Boston skyline, I quit thinking. I felt strange and wonderful all at once. I remembered something she told me about when she faced a crossroad in her life. She said that true crossroads only happen a few times in a lifetime but they do change the direction of one's life forever. Then it hit me square between the eyes. I was at that crossroads the old woman was talking about!

I had worked so very hard on The Coastal Cottage Inn for so many years. It was all I had for assets and income. So many wonderful things happen at the Inn. The Inn was my destiny. The Inn, and all my hard work was to show others what can be done when you followed your dreams. And they could do it, too. The Inn was a resting place for people going through some of the same events in life that I had gone through.

The ferry was slowing down, making its approach to the pier. As it got close to the shore, a creeping reality set in. I had called the bank to make arrangements for the mortgage payment on my inn. The woman who handled my loan told me over the phone, and then followed up with in a letter telling me that Congress had passed a new bill that was going to help people who were behind in the mortgage payments stay in their homes. She said under no circumstance should I make any more mortgage payments. I thought this odd but as she explained, the amount in arrears would be deferred and rolled into the note once the property was approved for the loan modification. Of course, I believed it was a blessing from God. I wouldn't have to make any payments, I could keep some money in the bank, and everything would fall nicely into place once the loan went through. Or so I was led to believe.

Days later, I was enjoying a busy summer and the Inn was full of guests. I had gone out to run a few errands and came home to find a note attached to my door. I could see that it was official and it filled me with a sense of dread as I yanked it off the door.

My hands shook as I read that my Inn was scheduled to be auctioned off - *in one week*! I called the woman who serviced my loan. She informed me that the loan modification did not get approved and that my home was sold 'in bulk' to another company, that they now held the mortgage on my inn and, despite previous instructions to not send in any more payments until the new loan was finalized, I was 'behind' on my mortgage payments, and was now 'in default.'

I was shocked and yet not surprised at the same time. I had come to know the evil ways of Corporate America very clearly. How could another company have my loan when I had a contract with them? She told me banks buy and sell loans all the time and this one was named Kondaur Capital in Orange, California.

Hmmmm, Kondaur... Sounds a lot like the predatory California Condor, doesn't it?

That evening, after keeping a smile on my face all day for my guests, I retreated to the attic where I had built myself a private bath chamber with exposed rafters and a chimney full of bricks and crumbling mortar. As I removed my clothes, I gently rubbed my hand on the crossbeam holding up the chimney; now, like me, I thought, so worn with age.

Before I settled into my bath, I had called my sister to tell her what was happening. I told her how scared I was of losing my home, my business, my Inn, and, if that wasn't traumatic enough, I had absolutely no place to go. That's what frightened me the most. I don't know what I expected her to say but I would have never called if I knew she'd respond.

"Well, you sure as hell can't come live with me!" Those were her exact words. I had never even considered it. It wasn't why I'd called. We were sisters. Maybe that meant something different to her than it did to me. And it wasn't the words that struck me so hard, it was the tone in her voice. It was a tone that said, 'I'm pretty damn happy in my own world and I don't need any charity cases.'

I lowered my body into the claw foot bathtub that faced two small arched windows overlooking the marina. I loved relaxing in the tub after a long day of playing innkeeper, feeling the bubbles smooth against my skin as I watched the sunlight or moonlight dance on the water below. That night, however, was not peaceful. It was the eleventh hour of my darkest day. As I sat in the tub reflecting on my situation, reality now touched my skin instead of warm, sudsy water. I had lost yet another home, my second little oasis I had enjoyed in my life. This time I couldn't blame my brother, I had to blame myself for believing the banks.

Laying in the comfort of my private chamber, I tried to relax but I couldn't get myself to take a full breath. The tightness in my chest was suffocating me. And the wine I had been drinking did not kill the emotional pain. Just the thought of having to pack up and load yet another moving van was overwhelming, particularly since I was being forced from the home I thought I would live in for the rest of my life, the home I would die in. The home I would leave to my sons.

The water had turned cold but I didn't care. The discomfort was somehow fitting.

Then my phone rang. It was Marcus. He had talked about marriage but I didn't know if I wanted that again. My life was at a crossroads.

"I can't look to a future any longer," I said. "I can't get excited about tomorrow."

He replied, "Then don't. I will lead you into tomorrow."

He was so sweet and so sincere, yet he knew my fears were well-founded. He told me to pack only the precious things. But I couldn't do that, I thought, all that was precious to me was my sons, my church, my sweet neighbor and dear friend, all of whom I would be leaving behind.

"I can't do it." I said.

"Yes, you can!"

In tears I repeated, "I have nowhere to go." I sat in the cold water, remembering how we met, thinking about Marcus and his encouraging words helped a lot. I quit crying, and gathered myself together and went back down to attend to guests.

When I bought my Victorian house in Hull, I invested all that was left of my share of my parent's estate; my share, that is, of what my brother felt I had coming to me after he bought his speed boat, snowmobiles, walk-in, heated, snowmobile trailer and God knows what else. I began to get angry at my brother again, but then quickly realized it was not his fault, it was mine. I wasn't really mad at him. I was mad at the world.

All that was left of the last 30 years of my life were memories. The memories of my life with my boys! The memories of my friends and their support when I'd finally established the Coastal Cottage Inn! The memories of the three moves - back and forth - in a rental truck between Salt Lake City and Boston just to make a stable life for me and my family! The only asset I'd have after losing my inn would be my Volvo, which was on its last leg. I wouldn't even have a job anymore. It was hard not to be bitter and I worked hard to count my blessings but, at that moment, all I could feel was loss.

Events in my life had shown me more than once that God has a plan, and the choice, once again, was mine. I knew what I needed to do. I needed to let go of the hurt, not focus on the bad and take that leap of faith into an unknown future once again. I needed to trust that all would be well, so I pulled myself together and said the words I still say today, "God Provides."

Days later, I received a phone call from a woman who was looking for a place to stay for one night only. She was on her way to New Hampshire on business and her hotel room in Boston was unexpectedly unavailable. She was from Colorado and was now stuck for a place to stay. Fortunately, one of my guests had cancelled at the last minute so I had a room open. I told her to take the ferry from Boston to Hull and I would pick her up at the dock.

A couple hours later I was loading her suitcase into the trunk of my Volvo S60. This car had saved my life once when I was broadsided by a woman traveling 50-mph in a 25-mph zone, but it was in pretty sad shape by then. The sunroof was permanently stuck open so I had to use a large black plastic garbage bags duct taped to the roof just to keep the rain out. Wouldn't you know, right after I picked up my overnight guest, it started to rain? The wind blew so hard it peeled the bag away from the tape in places and let in the rain. Goodheartedly, my guest happily helped me hold the plastic, duct-taped sheeting in place through while we drove back to the Inn. As we drove along, I told her that she was lucky she hadn't called later in the month, that I was closing the Inn and why. I was surprised about how much I shared with this stranger, and a guest, no less!

After we arrived at the Inn she commented on how beautiful it was and she went up to her room. A few minutes later she came out to the patio to join me and some of my other guests. It had stopped raining and we were enjoying the fresh night air, a glass of wine, and conversation. She poured herself a glass of wine and took an empty seat. After a bit, she looked at me seriously and said, "You can't lose this house! It's amazing!"

I told her there was not much I could do about it. She then informed me that she was in the mortgage business and asked me who was servicing my loan. When I told her the name of the company and the woman's name handling the account, she just about choked on her wine. She immediately picked up her cellphone and started to make a call. She said she had worked for the same company servicing my mortgage but had recently quit. And, more extraordinary, she was friends with the girl who had been trying to get me the loan modification. Everyone sitting on the patio, wine in hand were shocked at how incredibly coincidental this situation was.

When she got off the phone, she told us that my servicer had just sold a bulk of high equity loans to Kondaur Capital, the company that pushed the foreclosure. She suggested I call the Massachusetts Attorney General's office first thing in the morning.

"It's a scam," she said. "It's called equity skimming."

She explained exactly how equity skimming worked. She said that unscrupulous banks promise to refinance home loans that have a lot of equity, i.e. 'cash' in them. They then string the applicant along on the promised loan until they fall behind in the payments and into default. The companies then used the properties as tax write-offs (losses) until the foreclosed properties were sold in bulk and auctioned off. Not only would the finance company not take a loss, they would make money in the entire loss! It was a new way of stealing from homeowners and, despicably, making it appear to be the homeowner's fault. If a regular citizen did this it would be considered grand larceny. But for a bank and the insurance companies that were underwriting the 'risk' – it was considered a good business practice since it returned a profit to the stockholders.

I asked her to put everything she was relating in writing for me, which she did, and we exchanged email addresses.

After learning these details, Marcus and I went into high gear trying to save the Inn. Marcus jumped through hoops, calling and faxing complaint letters, trying to get through to the Attorney General to stop the foreclosure and the auction. I went to Congressman Delahunt's office with no success either. We filed a complaint with the bank, but the Commonwealth of Massachusetts told us their hands were tied. We filed a complaint with the Banking Federation but they could only mediate the complaint with Kondaur Capital if Kondaur agreed to sit down and discuss it! Well, that was stupid I thought. Why would the bank that just stole my home and made money doing, want to sit down to 'discuss it?' Does a mugger ever steal your wallet then call you on the phone to 'mediate" your complaint of a stolen wallet? The whole situation was abusive and intolerable.

Marcus even tried to buy the house from the scammers. He called in all his chips to purchase the house in a short sale, use his VA benefits for the purchase, contacted his bank, checked his credit score, talked with his financial advisor, etc. However, since my old Victorian home had three kitchens - one in the main house, one in the apartment, and one in a suite of rooms - the appraiser could not muster the imagination to appraise it as a single-family residence. Marcus was dumbstruck.

As the time got closer to the date of losing my home, my attorney was able to delay the July auction until October. The complaint stated something about the title being related to improper deeds. During the delay we contact everyone and anyone we thought could help undo this injustice. But, October arrived and the Attorney General of Massachusetts did nothing to help us. In the end, I lost my home.

Twelve days after I lost the house, the Massachusetts Supreme Court issued a ruling that *halted all foreclosures in the state* because of possible deed fraud throughout the industry; since there was serious doubt as to who actually 'owned' the titles of many foreclosed homes in Massachusetts, all mortgages and foreclosures were put on hold until mortgage companies could prove they held title to the properties. I missed keeping my beautiful home by a bureaucratic technicality, a 'policy' as it was described to me, and a mere ten 'business days.' To this day that phrase, 'business days,' has an ironic, bitter sound that lingers in the air like hydrogen sulfide gas every time I hear it.

Just before the bank took the house over, Marcus and I were quietly married across the street on the beach at sunrise; where I use to walk and talk with 'the Doc.' We hired Margaret, a Justice of the Peace, to meet us on the beach, and woke Christopher and Jonathan to come out and be our witnesses. It was simple, quiet, and sweet – all champagne and strawberries.

The boys went back to bed. Marcus and I packed. A week later it was all done.

My very own officer and gentleman on our wedding day.

Chapter 12: Living History

Unless someone pops in unexpectedly, Mrs. Washington and myself will do what I believe has not been [done] within the last twenty years by us, that is to set down to dinner by ourselves. – George Washington – 31 July 1797

Captain's Row

After I lost the Inn, the boys went to live in Nashville, and I moved to Virginia and transition into my new role as Marcus' wife. And, it was not lost on me that he was right; he did lead me into the future.

My new home, Marcus' circa 1940s condo, was small, so most of the twenty rooms of antique furnishings went into storage. After several months of paying storage costs, we estimated that we could find a larger home to rent and actually use my beautiful furnishings and be quite comfortable. And, as luck would have it, we found a fabulous old colonial home right on Captains Row on Prince Street in Old Town Alexandria.

The house was built in the 1790s, so, on moving day, we found that the only way to get our furniture to the fourth floor of the home was similar to the way they did it in colonial times - by using a jury-rigged pulley system, which ended up being my husband and three of his buddies with 100-foot ropes. Two of his friends were stationed on the 4th floor to retrieve the hoisted furniture, trying not to fall out of the French doors. Another hand was on the street kept tension on the messenger rope so that things going up didn't bang on the outside of the house or go through the historic windows. The last one hauled away on the pulley line taking the items to the top floor. It was quite a sight to behold and an ingenious engineering feat of those men.

My new home was so old, charming, and historic that while we lived there - *it literally started to fall apart*. After the earthquake in August of 2011 and Hurricane Irene two weeks later, the sewer lines to the house broke, the ancient bricks and mortar cracked and shifted, the chimney came undone and bricks smashed everything in the backyard as well as falling down the flue at night. There were horrid, septic smells in the kitchen that made eating in there very unpleasant. The landlords sent a repairman, but after the estimate, decided they didn't want to pay to have it fixed.

Luckily, one day, a city housing inspector just happened to be standing in front of our house, looking at the sewer lines that were being dug up for repair. I went out and asked him to come inside to see if he could smell what I had been smelling for the last six months. He took one whiff and said that it was definitely sewer gasses. He then ordered an investigation.

The stench was found to be coming from an old sewer pipe in the wall which had ruptured. The raw sewage had been seeping out and underneath the thin kitchen floor for years. For all we knew, we could have been smelling sewage from the Revolutionary War! The whole kitchen was declared unusable.

The repairmen dug up the floor and removed all the kitchen cupboards to get to the sewer lines. After they were fixed, however, the landlords had the sewage-soaked cabinets reinstalled just to save money. Then, to add insult to injury, after all the work was done and the sewer problem that plagued the house for years was fixed, the landlords refused to renew our lease. We were told to move. I suppose we were being punished for bringing the issue to the attention of the city housing inspector. So be it, we thought, and found a new place to live, one without sewer-soaked kitchen cabinets.

After moving four times in less than two years, Virginia proved to be a blessing in disguise. I found a great job working as a historical interpreter at Mount Vernon, George Washington's home. It was amazing that I, of all people, was working as a historical *anything*! Go figure! All I knew up to that point in my education was that George Washington was the first President, and something about chopping down a cherry tree. I was simply astonished that they would hire someone like me who knew absolutely nothing about George Washington! Of course, that was then, and this is now. I was trained by the most enthusiastic and knowledgeable people I had ever met and by the time they were done with me, I knew how to describe Washington's house, his family, and his life with the best of them. I used my hospitality background to make George

Washington's Mont Vernon visitors feel comfortable as they came into the rooms. During that time, a new history was made—mine!

I loved my twenty-minute commute to work, sunlit sparkles on the water as I drove along the Potomac River. The trees and birds were always on hand when I arrived in the mornings and the walk from the parking lot to the Mansion was like going to chapel, no one but me and God. George certainly was right when he said, "This home is situated on the best place on earth".

There are 540 acres of property in the estate. All the different trees, the birds, the vegetation, the smells that came from the earth, the way the sky changed color, the way the river's appearance continually changed, always beautiful, was absolutely heavenly to me.

The people I worked with were unlike any others I had met, there were people from all walks of life, many of them former teachers, professors, lawyers, military, military wives, and doctors. One of the volunteers was a retired general. We had stage actors, who were all very good, of all ages, personality types, and experience. They were young, old, quiet, and dynamic actors who, as 'first person interpreters,' easily got into the many colonial characters that had once visited Mount Vernon. We all got along very well and truly cared for each other. They were the sweetest, kindest group of people that ever gathered in one place, and we all *supported* one another.

Though I loved the job, it was not easy talking to 5,000 people each day and adhering to shift and tour schedules in order to make sure our co-workers were covered. We needed to provide smooth transitions for our 'guests' as they walked through the house, so everything needed to work like clockwork. It was challenging at times to coordinate all those people and maintain an orderly fashion.

Before moving to Virginia, I spent 50 years of my life dealing with tragedies. I always felt that it was just something I was destined to do, which was to struggle. But after landing in Virginia, I felt as though something else was happening in my life. It was a completely new experience, something I wasn't used to. In Virginia, at Mount Vernon, I lived in a perfect little world, and it felt strange to me. When I returned home from work after walking around the 500-acre plantation, my husband would massage my aching feet and sometimes run my bath so I could relax after a long day. And, if I didn't feel like cooking, he would take me to dinner. If I complained about a headache, a body ache, or that I didn't make it to the grocery store, he was ready, able, and willing to make sure I had no discomfort, or anything to complain about. He just wanted to make me happy.

When Marcus and I got married, Marcus joined my Church. He now attends three-hour church services with me on Sunday mornings. And, when I am too tired or more likely too lazy to go, he talks me out of it and into going to church. It is one thing to have a true ass for a husband; you have a good reason to gripe. But when you have someone who is at your beckon call, it is quite a different story.

The Doc was Right

My perfect new life took a stressful turn one day when I was at work upstairs at Mount Vernon. The house was busy and packed with tourists everywhere and we had gone on 'open door,' which meant that we had too many people to have them stop and listen as we gave them some interesting, historical facts. So, we would need to project our voices and repeat ass much information as possible as the tourists walked throughout the house.

This day I was in the in a tiny hall in what is called the 'Upper Hall,' and was in the midst of telling a large group about George Washington's death.

"This is the exact bed where George Washington died December 14, 1799," I tried to bellow. "After his death, Martha Washington never returned to this room. She retired up these stairs, to another suite, where she spent the rest of her days."

I suddenly began to feel odd, a bit funny. I started to realize that I was saying things incorrectly; my words weren't coming out right and I knew it.

I felt as though I should pick up the hand radio we used to contact with the staff and call for help, but my hand wouldn't move. I began to feel panic and to sweat. I knew *something was definitely wrong*. The house was on 'Open Door' which meant there were thousands of people coming through. We pretty much just tried to keep the line moving and would say a sentence or two while they moved along. But I could do nothing but stand there until a co-worker came to relieve me at the regular time, which was about ten minutes later.

After I was relieved of my post, I made my way to the employee break room. There were several people sitting down and enjoying some downtime between tours. I told my co-workers what had happened. I told them that something wasn't right and I should be checked out. My supervisor asked me questions about the episode I had experienced and said she thought it was just a momentary thing, not to worry about it. She sent me back to work.

On the short walk back to my station I called my nephew, who is a doctor. I told him what had happened and my symptoms. He told me to go to the emergency room *immediately,* that I might have had a stroke. When I went back to my supervisor, she insisted that I wait until 3:00 PM, which was an hour and half later. She said she couldn't let me leave because she needed to find someone to take my shift and stand outside on the front lawn and watch the people going into the house. Being a good employee, I stayed.

Marcus came to get me a 3:00 PM to drive me to the hospital. He had waited to come and get me, as instructed, but was pretty upset that I chose to do as my supervisor said. At the emergency room and after taking all my patient information, they wheeled me to the x-ray department to do some tests. When they got the results, they told me that I had had a Transient Ischemic Attack (TIA), or commonly known as a mini stroke.

Though it is never a good thing to have a TIA, I was lucky that it wasn't a more serious, incapacitating one. For almost two weeks I was an inpatient and outpatient at the hospital while they conducted a series of tests. I swear, I had every test imaginable. One of the physicians joked that if I didn't have the medical insurance that I did, I would never have had as many tests as I did. Though it was said as an offhanded joke, the fact of the matter is, the health care system had become so inflated that insurance companies stepped in to decrease costs to increase their stockholders' shares. But to make more money, the hospitals increased the sheer volume of tests and procedures; it was basic economics - the more tests they do - the more *they* get paid.

In those two weeks I had a cat scan, an MRI, and blood work that left me down a quart or two, EEGs, EKGs, heart monitoring, a stress test where they injected something nasty directly into my heart, and many other things too numerous to mention. I felt like the million-dollar woman, but without the bionics or Lee Majors.

At one point, one of the physicians wanted me to be admitted to the hospital again. When I got there, I found out that the reason for my hospital stay was so that they could do a urine test to determine if my adrenal gland was malfunctioning. He wanted me to stay for three days until they got the results back. It seemed insane to me and my other physician to charge the insurance company three days in the hospital just to pee in a bottle, So, after much coaxing, they released me to go home, where I could do the test at my leisure.

I took a brown bottle of liquid marked 'Nuclear Liquid' home with me. Over the next few days I collected the samples of urine and added them to the liquid. Without going into detail, it was time consuming and inconvenient and I was glad when it was over with. I took the bottle back to the hospital lab to be tested. The woman at the lab told me she couldn't accept my sample because it was ordered while I was *in the hospital* but was now an *outpatient* sample. She flatly refused to take it because they, the hospital, had no code to use for a test that was technically inpatient but was actually outpatient. I was shocked! I told the lab technician I wanted her to write down exactly what she had just said, verbatim, so I could take it up with the hospital administrator. She refused.

I was getting more and more frustrated by the lack of service and the lack of sense. I asked her to tell me what I should then do with the specimen in the large bottle labeled 'Biohazards' that I had been carting around with me for the last three days. Without the slightest interest or concern she said, "I don't know."

"Okay," I said. Then proceeded to tell her that I was going to take the hazardous waste out to the parking lot, dump it, and leave the bottle there. She immediately agreed to take it and told me that it would be tested. I walked out of there thinking I had the last laugh, until I called for the results.

A week had passed since I dropped the sample at the lab but I had not heard back from the doctor or the hospital, so I called. I spoke with a very polite woman on the phone who told me that there was no paperwork and no indication that a test had ever done. As I waited on the line, she searched their system but could not find any record of the sample or any lab results.

Shortly afterward, my doctor called. I told him the about the incident at the lab and the disappearance of my sample and results. He, too, was surprised. In the end, we found out that *the lab never did the test*, and when the medical staff asked me to come back into the hospital to repeat the test, I flatly, categorically, and positively refused.

For months after I still felt weird - that something was off.

My new cardiologist was from India. I sensed that he was getting as frustrated with the hospital as I was. He told me that there was one other test they should have been performed when I first presented with symptoms. He called it a table test. He explained that the table test would determine whether I had a problem with blood pooling, or Chronic Venous Insufficiency (CVI). After all, I did have a job where I was standing still most of the day. I was frightened and worried for days, wondering whether I needed surgery and a pacemaker.

When the day of the test came, the doctor explained the procedure in detail to Marcus and me. With the table test, the patient is placed on a bed that rotates from a horizontal position to a vertical position. If the patient faints or passes out, it indicates that they have a problem with the circulation in the legs. If the patient does not lose consciousness, then it indicates a heart arrhythmia, which requires surgery and a pacemaker. If I didn't pass out, he continued, he would immediately prep for surgery and I'd be in surgery for several hours. It was a very scary prospect and I suppose the fear showed in my eyes. As I was being strapped to the test bed, Marcus leaned over me, smiled and said, "I always did like you horizontal," then he kissed me tenderly, his big blue eyes reassuring me. When he left the room, I could still feel his lips on mine. The next thing I knew, I was waking up.

I awoke to a nurse and doctor beaming at me. I was groggy when Marcus entered the room, his smile and eyes warming me all over.

"What happened?" I asked.

"Well, pretty lady," the nurse said, "we rotated the bed and ten seconds later you passed out - COLD."

The doctor looked at me and said, "You do not need a pacemaker. You won't need one. No surgery for you." And with that news, I could feel my heart resume its patient rhythm.

In the end, they determined that I had not been drinking enough water at work and was dehydrated, which caused my hormone levels to fluctuate. Easy enough to cure but, apparently, not easy enough to diagnose. As it turned out, the hospital was taking full advantage of the insurance company, big time! My cardiologist, bless him, expressed his distaste for how the hospital managed health care, so much so, that one month later, he resigned his position at that hospital and moved his family back to India.

The whole ordeal reminded me of a conversation I had years ago with my supervisor at Beth Israel Deaconess Hospital in Boston. During one of those off-the-record employee chats, she confided that it was getting harder and harder for her to come into work. She said the meetings she attended were all about making more money, that the health of people had taken a back seat to the cash gods of privatized hospitals.

What I had experienced during my health scare, and believe is happening in the medical community today, is exactly what my friend, The Doc, was warning me about all those years ago during our walks on the beach.

God Provides – Does He Ever!

Marcus was working the weekends as a deckhand on the Alexandria Water Taxi, which transports people from one side of the Potomac River to the other. He was wanted to qualify for his 100-Ton US Coast Guard Captain's license, which required him to log ninety days on the water and take a boating course. The poor guy was taking orders, handling lines, and cleaning bathrooms (sorry 'heads') on the water taxi between Old Town and the National Harbor in Maryland. And just to show how insane and hoop driven this world can be, consider that he was a retired Navy Captain who piloted destroyers, large amphibious ships, and patrol boats for the Navy SEALS, but he couldn't pilot a yacht or a ferry without first getting a license from the Coast Guard. It was like saying you can be a pilot of a 747 but needed a special license to fly a Cessna. Crazy, huh?

One weekend, after I dropped Marcus off to work at the piers, I drove to Safeway to get my wine. As I walked up the aisle, I noticed a woman around my age getting her 'evening companion' as I jokingly called a bottle of vino. I scanned the shelf for the wine I usually bought and thought about how important wine had become to me, and to other women. It had a calming effect on us, especially those of us in menopause. Then I remembered a recent craving I had for Ruffles potato chips and sour cream with Lipton Onion Soup mix. And, since Marcus was at work, I could easily sit in front of the TV and watch the garbage they put on television and suck down some wine and chips just to see if I could get any fatter. I had gone from a size four to a size ten in just a little over a year, I deserved to go home and feel sorry for myself. Then I remembered what my sister told me once, "That's what *happy* looks like."

But I wasn't feeling particularly happy. The Church I had come to love had just been caught up in a horrible scandal, one that I could not bear to think about. When I first joined the Church I heard the rumors, but I had paid no attention because they were just that, rumors. The new allegations, however, came back more fierce and uglier. The sweet people I had come to know were being split apart like a buzzard's after a kill. Everyone had their own loyalties and beliefs and for some people, they clashed terribly. It was heartbreaking! Both sides claimed the split was due to heresy.

The cause of the scandal was the claim that the Elder Monk of the Monastery, Father Panteleimon, had been sexually molesting the younger monks for years. There were rumors that porn had been found in his skete[xii]. Even worse was the scathing indictment written and posted on the internet by one of the monks he allegedly molested as he was dying from cancer. I was so horrified by the accusations that it became a determining factor in my decision not go into the convent. Years before the scandal, Mother Thecla had told me that if I did join the convent, Father Panteleimon would eventually become my "master and commander." Unbelievably, this was also the same man who baptized my father when the spirit descended upon him and bathed him in a beautifully pure light.

Again, I was challenged in my resolve not to pass judgment. I absolutely believe that people are where they need to be, when they need to be there. God's will surely *will* be done. We can never see the whole picture of what God has planned for us. Each of us has to make our own way in the world and make our own mistakes, and hopefully, learn from them. We all have our own path, and in the end, it all weaves together according to God's plan in to the beautiful tapestry we call life. Maybe I wasn't supposed to become a nun and needed something dramatic to happen to help me choose the right course. Maybe the monk had some serious soul searching to do before he died. Maybe it was God's way of testing people's faith.

The problem lies in us as people who pray. We get too caught up in the person leading the service or the candles or the incense or the choir or the fundraiser or whatever we pick to worship, rather than the essence of the love, which is truly what it is all about in the first place. Christ, Himself, said not to follow any man. In keeping with that thought, I believe our priests, rabbis, ministers, and evangelists are there to help us find our way, just as our parents do. But they are like the rest of us, including our parents, not perfect. We all do the best we can.

Meanwhile, back at the monastery, some of the monks left the Church and started another, separate monastery, some priests from the parish houses sued the monastery for one of the churches they operated. Whole families in the congregation were torn apart.

And now they, *we,* were embroiled in the same sorted misbehavior as the Catholic Church! It was very traumatizing for us who loved their God and their Church. And it was personally hurtful to me.

After all was said and done, I chose to stay with Father Isaac, the priest who healed my son, and I prayed that the convent wouldn't break apart as well. And thank God, it didn't! For my part, I stayed out of the gossip as much as I could.

If I were the queen of the forest, which I'm not, I would have just given them the building they wanted. After all, Christ said, "If someone steals your cloak, give them your coat also." (Luke 6:29) And I think, and you can check me on this that, He was the one who also said, "Love thy Neighbor."

I've been to many churches and many denominations, but for me, the Greek Orthodox Church, as well as nature, the eyes of little children, and the sick, is where I feel like I'm closest to God. The truth was, we didn't need both buildings. God is not in the buildings. They are just buildings that house the people who worship. And I thought, no matter however beautiful the monastery (*and it is quite beautiful!*), it pales in comparison to God's love!

Over the years, there has been lots of talk about the collapse of the Greek economy, that there were backroom deals made at the most famous monastery on the Holy Mountain at Mt. Athos. It had been intimated that the Greece's economy fell due, in some part, to financial dealings of the Orthodox Church.

Regardless of the ongoing troubles, I attended my church because I loved God and Christ. I loved the chanting, the incense, and my little monks and nuns. I endured the in-fighting of Greek against Greek over allegiances of one church to another, monks threatening to sue monks, allegations of heresy, name-calling, and sexual misconduct. During that period of confusion and doubt, I tried not to judge them and continued going to church, ignoring completely the theological and political insanity erupting around me.

I had tried to forgive and forget about losing my homes, the betrayals of my ex-husband, other boyfriends, my employers, my family, and now this. It was as if they had all lost their minds and their hearts. They clearly had lost the true meaning of Christ and the Golden Rule; to love one another. The Beatitudes lay trampled, tarnished beyond recognition. And yet my faith endured.

No one, not even a Church could take that away from me.

Our first home on Prince Street in 'Old Town' Alexandria, Virginia

Father Isaac carrying the Gospel to services

Chapter 13: On the Waves of Change

Trust in the Lord with all your heart and lean not on your own understanding. – Proverbs 3:5

More Answered Prayers

While drowning my thoughts in my chardonnay, potato chips and sour cream, I re-examined every moment trying to find the one common denominator for why things have happened the way they have. A person could go crazy trying to unravel a lifetime, trying to find the stitch that sent the whole thing askew. When I focus on certain events or outcomes, I begin asking myself some pretty painful questions. Was it something I said or something I didn't say? I wonder, did I not give enough? Did I give too much? And, what would have happened if I did this instead of that, would the end be the same? But, in the end, it is nothing more than poking and picking at old wounds.

I think about my sons, Christopher and Jonathan, and all we've been through together. The moves, the hospital visits, the funerals, the baseball and football games, school work, guitar lessons, rollerblades, business ideas, girlfriends, boyfriends, the Easter bunny and Santa Claus.

When Jonathan was just a baby, I noticed that he had been born with the gift of perfect pitch. His first crib toy was a little clown that played Beethoven. He played that tune over and over and over again. He was also born with the gift of 'Blarney' which he inherited from his very Irish-and-proud-of-it father, Jimmy. He never failed to make me laugh on our long drives when he would throw his voice and change characters. How was so very gifted at capturing the essence of a thing. He would dissect all the distractions around a subject and go straight to the truth. When his school did standardized testing, they found his comprehension skills to be at a college grade level. He was eight years old and in third grade.

Today, Jonathan is a great musician. It makes me happy to listen to him play guitar. He had taught himself to play after we moved into the Coastal Cottage Inn in Hull. I wasn't aware at the time, probably because I was busy getting my inn up and running, but the area had a seedy element to it. Just down the road was a housing project that was infested with drugs. Jonathan, being new to town, had befriended some boys in school that lived in the project.

One day I had come home from work to find him absolutely stoned out of his mind. His new pals, being the generous sort of guys druggies are, had given him a joint, marijuana that is. I was livid and scared, and we had quite a to-do over it, though he was really too stoned to argue coherently - so I grounded him for over a month.

It was difficult for him to be so isolated and difficult for me to see him so unhappy. But I knew it was better to separate him from those boys sooner rather than later, after the relationships had cemented. I know now that it was one of the best decisions I had every made as a parent. It kept him away from those particular bad influences and, as a result of his home imprisonment, he taught himself to play an excellent guitar during his incarceration

When Jonathan turned twenty years old he moved from Utah to Nashville to live with Christopher who ended up there by following a girlfriend who thought that's where she wanted to live. After a week or two, she left. Chris stayed and I thought it would be good for Jon to be in the music capital of the world where he could live out his dreams of being a musician. Christopher finally, was touching his art, literally as a tattoo artist on Broadway and making good money at it.

During this Nashville period, Chris had informed me that a girl he dated one night was pregnant and I was to be a grandmother. Wonderful news, for sure, but the not-so-wonderful news was that the mother of my son's child was addicted to OxyContin®, a very powerful and highly addictive opiate pain medication. My mind raced with thoughts of my unborn grandchild in the womb of a woman in drug rehab; my son trying to hold her and himself together, while helping his brother who was badly abusing alcohol.

I wished I possessed the power to make them see what a dangerous path they were both on. The dark, seedy, alcohol and urine-soaked streets of Nashville, the limitless availability of bars and scantily-dressed girls, snorting and injecting who knows what!

Thank God yet again! Shortly after Chris delivered his *you're-going-to-be-a-grandmother* news announcement, he called to inform me that the drug-addicted girl WAS NOT carrying his child but another man's, she was just trying to make the other man jealous with a tryst with Chris. Good news for sure yet another child was going to be born to yet another messed-up mother and would be reared by two people not ready or equipped to be parents.

Early one morning, however, I awoke to several messages blinking insistently on my phone. I dialed into my voicemail to retrieve them. They were from Chris. He said that Jonathan had been taken to the hospital for alcohol poisoning. He, evidently, had been drinking heavily the night before and had been found in a back corner of a parking garage, laying in his own vomit. Thankfully, he was seen in the emergency room and released. There was nothing for me to do, Christopher just wanted me to know.

The following year Jonathan had sunk to even lower levels. He had moved out of Chris's apartment and was living in an area close to the train tracks where the homeless and soulless were gathering. He was posting on Facebook saying that Satan was in control. He was terrifying me, but never gave up. I knew God had answered my prayers for Christopher so surely, he would for Jonathan. I pulled out all the stops. I called the Monastery for prayers. I found a book of prayers myself for exorcisms and lit candles in my chapel with a photograph of Jonathan propped next to them. I surrounded his picture with icons of John the Baptist, the Virgin Mary, and a photograph of his deceased grandparents. I then called upon all the angels I could muster and prayed that he would find enlightenment. I did that for days on end.

A memory of Johnathan played over and over in my mind. I was standing at the kitchen sink doing dishes and screaming at the boys to pick up their toys. My sweet little two-year-old boy came running over in his diaper and stood at my side. His angelic little eyes looked up at me sweetly, his outstretched chubby little arms begged for a hug and pierced through my anger with these words, "I love you, Mommy." I then wished I could pierce through his alcohol addiction and through his pain with just those same powerful words – "I love you."

Later that night, I went upstairs to my little home chapel. I was full of pain, fear, and anxiety. There is nothing worse than watching your children choose the wrong path, and knowing fully well where that path leads. I felt as though my body had been pushed to the limits of its endurance yet once again. It was, in essence, another glimmer of hell. I was actually physically symptomatic. I was unable to catch a full breath. My chest was tight and painful. I experienced a burning sensation throughout my body as if my nerves were out of control and pulsating. The pulsating nerves made me sick to my stomach. My brain frantically pounded on my skull to escape, which blurred my vision. I began to see blind spots and jagged white lines. I felt so awful emotionally and physically. I had no idea what was happening. Afterward, when I related the experience to a friend, she said she had a similar experience. It was brought on by extreme stress.

 I had recently come across Dahn Yoga[xiii] and was using the techniques to calm my mind and body down. I thumped on my chest and shook my shoulders up and down. I tapped my intestines where people hold all the toxicity in their bodies, which made sense since that's where we process and eliminate waste. I tried to bring my heart, mind, and soul into a state of equilibrium. But, truthfully, nothing was helping. As I went to kneel on my 18th century prayer bench, I found my knees on the floor instead of the knee pad, and my head, instead of upright, was lying on the arm pad with my arms dangling over the front of it. I had literally collapsed in front of the iconostas[xiv]. I was too tired to stand or kneel at my prayer station. I was beyond exhausted.

 As I started to pray for my sons, I recalled the famous depiction of an angel draped over a tomb. All that can be seen of the angel are its glorious wings flowing behind it, the arms draped, and a head held in a desperate pose, totally exhausted from trying to save the person who had died and was buried there. And that is how I felt. That, I thought, is me, clinging to my sons, and clinging to my dead, suicidal husband. And now, some 20 years after that battle was lost, a text messaged photograph of my son lying in a puddle of his own vomit, tattoos covering most of his body, piercings in his face, the ambulance taking him away. Another text came in of Jonathan lying in the hospital bed, those same arms that I knew back then hanging limp by his side, an IV drip trying to revive him.

 I tried to take the blame or even find the blame. I wanted to understand what had happened to make this the outcome of my life's work. I searched my memory and tried to figure out what I had done wrong. Where had I failed them? Did I work too much? Did I try too hard to get them to believe in God? Should I have made them go to church and become altar boys? Did I date too much, move too many times, and say the wrong things to them at the wrong time? What was that singular event or cumulative effect of my life that made the people I loved go down paths I never, ever wanted or intended?

I tried to identify all the rights I did instead of the wrongs. I went to all the school programs and always tried to keep clean and fashionable clothes on them so the other kids wouldn't single them out or make fun of them. I even quit a job once because they would not allow me come in late so that I could go see Christopher's first school recital. I made sure they always received what they wanted at Christmas time. I tried to support them in team sports—hockey, football, soccer, t-ball, and baseball - and I went to most games and practices. I went to the school concerts and school plays. I did all those things the child development experts tell us make for well adjusted, well round children. So, what did I do so wrong that all they wanted to do is sleep all day, party all night, and chase after money and women? My life to me was, and is, a mystery and I feel like the perpetrator, the detective, and the victim of the crime.

I leaned prostrate on my prayer bench, I gave my soul, thoughts, and feelings totally over to God. As I handed over myself to Him, once again, God heard my prayers. I prayed, "Father, if this is thy will, at least remove my pain." I prayed more earnestly and I felt totally isolated in the fear of where my boys were headed. Yet through my experience deep down I had complete confidence that I was being held by the Father even if it were in the flames of fear. I one again, gave my will to God. Then, I handed Him the souls of my children.

I had to remind myself that I had done all I could do and now, as hard as it may be, I had to let go. As Gibran once wrote,

Your children are not your children; they are life's longing for itself. They come though you into the world but they are not from you. You can house their bodies but not their souls."

I let it go and felt peace.

The peace, once again, I felt at that moment, came from the knowledge that we are all energy and that nothing can or should be judged. I found strength in Khalil Gibran's philosophy that through suffering, everyone is on his or her own journey. The question as a parent is, how do you move off the road they are on - no longer supporting them financially, with advice, or by example - and yet keep them in your heart?

The next time my husband and I were visiting the boys in Nashville, after the emergency room episode, we took Jonathan out to dinner. We were having a pleasant visit, eating fine food and having good conversation. After a while, Jonathan pulled out his wallet, removed something, and handed it to me. When I looked in my hand, it was a silver cross and religious medal. I recognized the cross as the one he had gotten from the monastery in Massachusetts many years ago, and a little medal given to him by my sister-in-law. She had given it to him for protection. I burst into tears when I saw them. I thought my boys had given up on God long ago. From that moment, I resolved that I will take comfort in the knowledge that he has them in his wallet. And, if nothing else, I have given him the awareness of an alternate path to walk - if he so chooses.

Christopher ultimately moved back to Utah and convinced Jonathan to join him in selling nutraceutical vitamins for a startup company Le-Vel. It is a lifestyle transformation plan and it became the answer to my prayers. Both boys are now fully engaged in trying to better their health and more importantly, their way of life. The company focuses on positive thinking, positive planning, and being there for others. I think their success in changing their lives was a combination of the vitamins cleaning out their systems, so they could think more clearly, and the encouragement to change their lives for the better. They seem to now have a new direction in life, one that focuses on what is good and right, rather than dark and despairing.

I watched as they both changed in remarkable ways. Jon started posting positive, remarkable things on his Facebook page instead of satanic rants. He is a totally different man than the one who was floundering in Nashville. He became a hero to hundreds of people he helped with his new vocation.

In fact, they both were doing amazing things. They have a following of people who are trying to change their lives for the better.

Christopher has found that charity is the best use of extra cash and has given thousands of dollars to the less fortunate. Jonathan's special focus is talking to people about taking control of their lives and getting rid of their addictions. They are now both earning seven-figure incomes. *Success* Magazine ran a two-page article about Christopher and his achievement with his new vocation. Though I prayed and hope, and prayed some more, even I, their mother, could not have dreamed that they would change so drastically and become so successful in such a short time. I feel that we all have been blessed.

Their Mother's and Father's Day gift to us in 2015 was an all-expenses paid vacation to Cabo San Lucas, Mexico for exceeding their sales quotas. We had a glorious time in the sun! And, if that isn't enough, that Christmas they surprised us with a BMW 550i and made a beautiful video of the surprise, thanking us for being there for them through thick and thin. UNBELIEVABLE how God works for those who have faith in Him.

I have found that prayers are extremely powerful, especially those of a mother! I have unexplained experiences which may or may not be scientifically verifiable. For those who need to see evidence with their eyes instead of taking someone's word for it, watch a video, <u>Down the Rabbit Hole</u>, from the Heart Math Institute. The basic premise is that the heart receives information before the brain does. A prayer of heart and compassion being sent from one person to another has powerful consequences and outcomes. And for those of you who need more scientific evidence, look into the research of Masaru Emoto on the effect of prayers have on water molecules.

The world is a fascinating place and we should all be thankful to be living in it, and pray for those who find it full of pain. I can attest that pain can be overcome by love. Start by loving yourself and respecting yourself.

Then, ask God for help and watch what happens!

Sea Story

Marcus grew up an Army brat, moving from place to place, where ever his father's assignment took him. He lived in many countries overseas and in different towns all across United States. Through his travels, he developed a virtuous image of his country, a country he thought worthy of defending, so he joined the Navy. As a Naval Officer, he was responsible for the security, safety, and welfare of his shipmates, and he took that duty quite seriously.

When he retired from the Navy and got a job as a defense analyst, he found out quickly that in the private sector wasn't about honor or country, *it was all about profits*, and it ran cross-purposes and counter to his view and philosophy of life when he was in the Navy. The years in his civilian career showed him just how various organizations in the Department of Defense exemplified the phrase 'show me the money.' They would develop new weapons systems and equipment and hire companies in the private sector to support the work.

In a clear example of the right hand not knowing what the left hand was doing, he saw multiple agencies within the DoD doing similar work to develop similar systems, without any concern about the duplication of efforts or redundancy. The taxpayers had no idea that they were paying for parallel efforts, several times over, from different pots of money. It was ludicrous, wasteful, and financially insensitive to the people who worked so hard to provide support for their families and their country.

It got to the point where he absolutely dreaded going to work. He hated his job with its politics and lunacy. Despite his years of service and knowledge of how to protect sailors and their ships, he felt he was being sidelined, marginalized by bureaucrats who 'had never walked point' or, as he often said, "They just don't get it. They've never stood the mid-watch."

He was always looking for something new to do. Yet, he hung on, pushing through the mercenary mire of his job, his enthusiasm waning with every hour, all the while getting emotionally and physically weaker, his spirit starting to fade from gray to black.

When he started to believe me about choosing the right thoughts and emotions to carry around with us each day, he moved into a good place. He got a new job and is enjoying its challenges. He started to enjoy doing theatre again and was nominated 'Best Actor in a Musical' for a production of the musical, "Dirty Rotten Scoundrels" in 2015 and 'Best Actor in a Drama' in 2017 for "Taking Sides" in Motif Magazine, the Rhode Island arts magazine. He serves on two municipal board for the city of New London, CT and is an active sculptor again.

I knew the tide had turned a few months ago when he gave me the greatest compliment I've ever had; "Honey, my mother gave me birth - but *you* have given me life.'

Before: Jon and Chris 'appearing' at the Ryman Auditorium in Nashville - One night only.....

After: Chris (L) and Jon (RC) with Le-vel founders Jason Camper (LC) and Paul Gravette (R) at La Caille restaurant in Salt Lake City, the same restaurant where I used to wait tables as a single mother.

Chris and Jonathan on the Jumbo-tron at the Le-vel Awards where Jonathan received the $1 Million in sales award.

Chapter 14: Revelations

Blessed are the pure in heart for they shall see God. – Matthew 5:8

It might have appeared to be an unusual question out of the blue but I needed to ask the Bag Lady, "Were you a nun?" She seemed to be such a spiritual person that it made perfect sense to me.
She didn't answer.
Where do you go in the winters?" I asked.
She just looked at me.
After a long silence she began talking about the Jesus Prayer; continually repeating His name. She said it had become more precious and sweet to her than anything in the world. At times, she went on, she would walk twenty miles in a day but did not feel like she was walking at all. She was only aware of repeating the Jesus Prayer over and over again. When the bitter cold pierced through her clothes, she would say her prayer more earnestly, then become warm all over. When hunger began to overcome her, she called on the name of Jesus and would forget her wish for food. When she fell ill and got rheumatism in her back and legs, she fixed her thoughts on her prayer and did not notice the pain.

"If anyone harms me," she said, "I have only to think, how sweet the prayer of Jesus is, and the injury and anger pass away."

It occurred to me that she had become a half-conscious person, having no cares and no interests. All the fussy business of the world wasn't worth a passing glance to her. She wanted to be alone in her prayer with Jesus. It was the one thing she lived for in life and the only thing that gave her tremendous joy.

She then told me how she moved to the streets and traveled around to different places, but her home, she said, was where ever Jesus was, and that as long as she had her prayers as her companion, she had everything she needed. Her prayers heartened and consoled her throughout her journeys and with other people she'd meet. As she got older, however, she decided it would be better for her to stay in one place. She prayed constantly wherever she ended up. Her shelter was her prayer. And that is how I found her in the park.

"Christ is my Church. God is my strength," she told me.

Inside I thanked God and pondered His mysterious power, which He gives His creatures; dry, putrid ones, almost brought to dust, and yet keeping such vital force, and giving life to others who are dead in their spirit. The human soul is not bound by place and matter. It can see, even in the darkness, what happens in the distance, as well as things near at hand. Often, we do not give force and scope to this spiritual power; instead we crush it beneath the yoke of our gross bodies or diminish it with our haphazard worldly thoughts and ideas. But when we concentrate within ourselves, when we draw away from everything around us and become subtler and refined in mind, then the soul comes into its own, and works to its fullest power.

She then asked me how I came to live in Boston.

"Was it a coincidence," she asked rhetorically, "that we met and that we had so many things in common?"

She smiled and I drew closer to her, being pulled by the warmth of her gaze and the serenity of her smile.

As I looked deep into her dawning eyes, her face slowly but gently started to change. As it moved and reshaped I began to see something familiar in the vision that reformed in front of me. I couldn't put my finger on it initially but as time went on, I realized that I was looking at a near mirror-image of my own face blended with the face of the old Bag Lady. Soon I saw that same face I had stared at for years as an awkward, embarrassed, bullied child, the face as an abused young woman, the exhausted gaze of a young struggling mother raising two boys, the bemused air of an aspiring model applying her make-up, the crushed look of a deserted wife and lover, the gritty leer of a determined woman fighting for survival in a man's business world, and, finally, the contented air of a loved, protected, confident woman in the arms of her loving husband and family. I stared in astonishment at the blending face in front of me and then I found myself smiling a smile matching her brilliant beam.

Then her face returned again to the vision I had known all these years, and, still smiling, she turned and walked slowly away, almost floating across the Boston Common and disappeared as wistfully as she had appeared.

I never saw her again.

Though, I chat with her often, in prayer.

Epilogue

Don't cry because it's over; smile because it happened. – Dr. Seuss

    We had a full day ahead. It was early morning and there was beautiful blue sky and fairly calm breeze off Long Island Sound. Marcus had written a play for the local Greek Church in town based on the parable in the Bible, "The Seed Sower." It was to be performed that very afternoon for the congregation.
    Before we did that, however, Marcus and his brother, Nelson, were going to do a burial-at-sea with their father's remains off the back of our boat in Long Island Sound on the Connecticut shoreline. While they set up an area in the boat to read prayers and scatter the ashes in the water below, I sat on the sofa in the salon, with my Bible in hand, close to my heart, and closed my eyes. I then asked the Lord, which I frequently do, what my message for the day will be. When I opened the book to a random page, my message was;

*   And when he was alone, those who were about him with the twelve asked him concerning the parables. And he said to them, "To you has been given the secret of the kingdom of God, but for those outside everything is in parables; so that they may indeed see but not perceive, and may indeed*

hear but not understand; lest they should turn again, and be forgiven." And he said to them, "Do you not understand this parable? How then will you understand all the parables? The sower sows the word." - Mark 4:10-14

We get what we sow; by the friends we choose to be around, the music we listen to, the movies we watch, down to the very thoughts we think; EVERYTHING has energy, both good and bad. We are getting what *we choose to get*.

I have realized that my college professor was right. I got the things on my wish list from all those years earlier:

✝ By the grace of God, Christopher and Jonathan are finding themselves and helping others along the way. Both have kind, giant hearts.

✝ I have gotten even closer to God and witnessed many actual miracles and almost became a nun myself.

✝ I had purchased a 20-room Victorian home on the Atlantic Ocean across the bay from Boston Harbor. It was, in fact, 20 miles from Harvard!

✝ I am married to a warm and very loving man.

✝ I have another beautiful Victorian and just opened the Coastal Cottage Inn (II) and I am financially stable.

Many people who have watched my life unfold would often say, "You can't make this shit up!"

My advice: Try to be kind to others when people aren't so kind to you in return. Perhaps their actions may be shrouded opportunities to make us better. We get to choose whether it does or not. It doesn't matter if you go to a church, a mosque, a wat, a pagoda, a temple, a synagogue, or do tribal dancing. What is important is that we be kind to one another. Don't hurt people. And Love your neighbor as yourself! *Do unto others as you would have them do unto you.* Be very mindful that if you don't take care of yourself and love yourself, you won't be able to value others.

In the past five years we have traveled visiting Italy, Croatia, Spain, Ireland, Germany, Jamaica and Puerto Rico twice.

We recently bought a beautiful 42-foot classic Grand Banks trawler ADAGIO and cruise the Long Island shoreline. In the coming years we will cruise to Boston, Maine, and south to Chesapeake Bay and magical Annapolis, where our love affair took flight.

Once we master that, we plan on making a Caribbean run and then...

...see where the ADAGIO takes us.

Our trawler ADAGIO at the Naval Submarine Base Marina

The Coastal Cottage Inn (II) New London, CT

Endnotes

[i] Hull, MA is a town on a small peninsula in Boston Harbor off the Atlantic coast.

[ii] At the beginning of the century, thousands of young Greeks began coming to Utah to live their first years of exile in a new land. Like myriad Greeks since ancient times, forced to leave their rocky land that could not sustain them, they vowed to return within a few years. Any life outside PATRIDHA, "the fatherland," was exile. Not knowing what the three MOIRCI, "the Fates," had decided for them during their first three days of life, many brought a bit of earth in an amulet or small bottle. If their destiny was death in American exile, a priest would have a pinch of Greek earth to sprinkle over them as they lay in their caskets. (Utah_history_website)

[iii] The Spanish Steps are a set of steps in Rome, Italy, climbing a steep slope between the Piazza di Spagna at the base and Piazza Trinità dei Monti, dominated by the Trinità dei Monti church at the top. The Scalinata is the widest staircase in Europe

[iv] The Mysteries: a religious belief based on divine revelation, especially one regarded as beyond human understanding.

v Dr. Lori Steinberg was a former nun, though I suspect, once a nun, you're always a nun.

vi Blessed St. Xenia was a "fool-for-Christ," who, for 45 years, wandered the streets of St. Petersburg, Russia. For the first 26 years of her life, Xenia had lived quite comfortably. However, after her husband suddenly died, the Holy Spirit led her to give away all her possessions to the poor. She put on her dead husband's clothes and called herself by his name, saying that Xenia had died. Homeless, she lived in the streets year-round for 45 years, owning only the ragged clothes on her back. The Holy Spirit also led her to give away her mind and her heart to God. By giving everything away, she became rich in humility, simplicity, self-denial, kindness, and deep and profound love for all. By pretending to be insane, she showed how insane the world and its values are. By denying herself the comforts of a home, a bed, decent clothes, food, and the appearance of being "normal," she helps us to examine what really is important in life, and what really is "normal." She trusted totally that God would provide for her, as He provides for the birds.

During the day she wandered the streets, dressed in rags, enduring heat and cold, snow and rain, mocked by people. At night she went out into the fields and prayed all night, and at other times she spent the night at the Smolensk Cemetery. It was at this cemetery that she helped the workmen build the Church of the Smolensk Icon of the Mother of God, by secretly carrying bricks up the scaffold during the night. One night the workmen hid to find out who was helping them, and discovered that it was "crazy Xenia." Whenever someone gave her alms, she immediately gave it to the poor. As the years passed, the Holy Spirit filled Xenia with greater riches, and she became increasingly blessed. After a while, some people started to notice that "crazy Xenia" wasn't so crazy after all, but was an instrument of divine grace, to whom had been given deep spiritual powers: she could see into people's hearts and into the past and future, and appeared to people in visions. Anyone whom she touched was blessed. Because she gave up living for herself, she was able to live for others, helping those in need. She especially helped families, children and marriages, as she continues to do today.

After she died around 1803, she continued to help those who prayed for her assistance. Throughout the 19th century, tens of thousands of people came every year to her grave, and countless miracles occurred. In 1902 a chapel was built over her grave in the Smolensk Cemetery, located on the western end of Vasiliev Island in St. Petersburg. This chapel has now been reconstructed, welcoming the pilgrims who come there every day, and the miracles continue to occur. For 200 years people have turning to the Blessed One, and she has been helping them. Her great spiritual power and her deep love for people transcend the grave and are manifested daily. _Life of St. Xenia of Petersburg_ by Jane M. deVyver – Internet download.

[vii] Practicing strict self-denial as a measure of personal and *esp.* spiritual discipline. <u>Merriam-Webster Dictionary</u> © 1979.

[viii] A lifestyle pursuing spiritual goals.

[ix] The Church of the Holy Sepulcher, also called the Basilica of the Holy Sepulcher, or the Church of the Resurrection by Eastern Christians, is a church within the Christian Quarter of the walled Old City of Jerusalem. The site is venerated as Golgotha [1] (the Hill of Calvary), where Jesus of Nazareth was crucified.

[x] Julian Calendar – Named after Julius Caesar in 45 BC, consisted of eleven months of 30 or 31 days and a 28-day February (extended to 29 days every fourth year), and was actually quite accurate: it erred from the real solar calendar by only 11½ minutes a year. After centuries, though, even a small inaccuracy like this adds up. By the sixteenth century, it had put the Julian calendar behind the solar one by 10 days. In 1582, Pope Gregory XIII ordered the advancement of the calendar by 10 days and introduced a new corrective device to curb further error: century years such as 1700 or 1800 would no longer be counted as leap years, unless they were (like 1600 or 2000) divisible by 400. If somewhat inelegant, this system is undeniably effective, and is still in official use in the United States. The Gregorian calendar year differs from the solar year by only 26 seconds—accurate enough for most mortals, since this only adds up to one day's difference every 3,323 years. Despite the prudence of Pope Gregory's correction, many Protestant countries, including England, ignored the papal bull. Germany and the Netherlands agreed to adopt the Gregorian calendar in 1698; Russia only accepted it after the revolution of 1918, and Greece waited until 1923 to follow suit. And currently many Orthodox churches still follow the Julian calendar, which now lags 13 days behind the Gregorian.

[xi] Bishop (Archimandrite) Goury was an Orthodox Priest who spent many years on a mission to Beijing, China where he translated the New testament into Chinese.

[xii] Skete - A monastic community in Eastern Christianity that allows relative isolation for monks, but also allows for communal services and the safety of shared resources and protection. It is one of four early monastic orders along with the eremitic, lavritic and coenobitic that became popular during the early formation of the Christian Church.

[xiii] The best way to describe Dahn Yoga exercises is as a blend of traditional yoga, tai chi and martial arts. It focuses on a person's physical, emotional, and spiritual well-being.

[xiv] Iconostas or Iconistasis - A screen or wall which serves as a stable support for

icons and marks the boundary between the nave and the altar or sanctuary.

www.ingramcontent.com/pod-product-compliance
Lightning Source LLC
Chambersburg PA
CBHW051753040426
42446CB00007B/340